Keep Law Alive

Keep Law Alive

James Boyd White

CAROLINA ACADEMIC PRESS

Durham, North Carolina

Library of Congress Cataloging-in-Publication Data

Names: White, James Boyd, 1938– author.
Title: Keep law alive / James Boyd White.
Description: Durham, North Carolina : Carolina Academic Press, LLC, 2019.
Identifiers: LCCN 2019003160 | ISBN 9781531015077 (alk. paper)
Subjects: LCSH: Law—United States. | Law—Philosophy.
Classification: LCC KF389.W45 2019 | DDC 340/.1—dc23
LC record available at https://lccn.loc.gov/2019003160

e-ISBN: 978-1-5310-1508-4

Carolina Academic Press
700 Kent Street
Durham, North Carolina 27701
Telephone (919) 489-7486
Fax (919) 493-5668
www.cap-press.com

Printed in the United States of America

To Mary

Contents

Acknowledgments

IT IS A REAL PLEASURE to be able to thank the following friends, who generously read and criticized this book, or parts of it, in draft: Walter Brueggemann, Richard Dawson, Julen Etxabe, Jeanne Gaakeer, Sarah Higinbotham, Martha Jones, John McCausland, Julian Davis Mortenson, Jeffrie Murphy, Pauline Phoa, Jefferson Powell, Jack Sammons, Barry Sullivan, Winnifred Sullivan, Jacobien van Dorp, Joseph Vining, Robin West, and Mary White.

Parts of each chapter have been published elsewhere in somewhat different form and are here reprinted by the kind permission of the publishers. Versions of chapters one and two appeared in "Legal Knowledge," 115 *Harvard Law Review* 1396 (2002); an earlier version of chapter three appeared in "What's Wrong with Our Talk about Race?," 100 *Michigan Law Review* 1927 (2002); a rather different form of chapter four appeared in "An Old-Fashioned View of the Nature of Law," 12.1 *Theoretical Inquiries in Law,* paper 13 (Tel Aviv University) (2010); an earlier version of chapter five appeared in "Law, Economics, and Torture," in *Law and Democracy in the Empire of Force,* 265, (edited by me and Jefferson Powell, 2009); parts of chapter 6 appeared in "Augustine's *Confessions* as Read by a Modern Law Teacher," 29 *Journal of Law and Religion* 330 (2014); other parts of that same chapter use material from "The Word and the Law," 41 *Georgia Law Review* 923 (2007), including excerpts from a play by François Ost, *Antigone Veiled* (2004).

I am grateful to Carolina Academic Press for the remarkable cover to this book, which is worth attention. It not only has a beautiful and provocative design, it is founded upon a photograph that has thematic connections with the book itself. The photo is a picture of the Capitol building in Washington, which we were told was taken in 1865 or thereabouts. That was the year of Abraham Lincoln's second Inauguration, during which he would have given his Second Inaugural Address from the steps we can see in the picture, a moment in our history of which we can all be proud.

A note for the reader: you will notice that sometimes books are cited in the footnotes with no designation of the author, and in those cases, I was the author.

Foreword

MY IDEA IN THIS BOOK is to express my sense of what law is like at its best—how it works, what it offers us, what it requires of us, both as lawyers and as citizens, and what it would mean to lose it. I want to do this at this time in history because, as I say immediately below, I think the law as we know it is subject to serious threats today, threats I elaborate both explicitly and implicitly in the body of the book.

1

The book begins with an immersion in legal thinking of a kind I believe to be of a high and traditional order, and ends with the recognition of another sort of thinking and being which I think may help us live with and respond to the threats I mention.

In it I speak from a world—the world of law and democratic government in which I grew up and was educated and led most of my working life—that is now in peril in our country. This world was built upon the imperfect but real assumption that our polity is a constitutional democracy, based upon a fundamentally reliable electoral process, and that, with all its defects—some of them serious indeed—law is an institution that should be treated with utmost respect as an essential and valuable part of our public world.

My concern here is not with the fundamental features of the rule of law—such as a democratically elected legislature, an independent judiciary committed to respecting authorities external to itself, the requirement that laws be public, the existence of checks and balances designed to ensure that power is not concentrated in one person or one institution, the principle of habeas corpus that no person should be detained without judicial review of his or her case, the basic requirements of due process of law, the idea of a commonwealth of shared values and interests, the sense that at the heart of every legal case is the question of justice—although every one of these principles is foundational and under serious threat.

A principle I do elaborate is the idea that the work of the judiciary should consist of responsible engagement both with the range of authoritative texts and practices that bear upon the case and with the reality of the world in which the decision will have its life—that is, both with what is commonly called the law and with justice itself. For at the heart of every legal case is the question of justice. As I say in chapter five,[1] I think the Supreme Court of the United States is in danger of losing its commitment to that principle. If so, it will lose its dignity and value as a court as well, becoming just another arena in which political battles are fought out without real regard either to law or to justice.

My aim in this book is not so much to develop the points just made, important though they are, as to define the complex intellectual, ethical, and emotional life at the heart of the law, the life by which the principles I identify are themselves given their life and definition. We could after all have a legal system in which all those principles were nominally affirmed, but which was so crude and thoughtless in its work that they did not in the end mean much after all.

What kind of thinking and writing gives these principles real life? My own sense is that what law calls for in those who practice it, or teach it, or live with it in other ways, is at heart an art, an art of language and composition. The law in this living sense is not just a set of rules or institutions, but an activity of the mind and imagination—a form of life—that has the value of justice at its heart.

What I say here about law is meant to be an expression of basic fealty and respect, both for what the law has been and what it can be. It is necessarily my own version of the life of the law that is recorded here. I am speaking about law as I learned it and practiced it and taught it. I know

1. See "The Disappearance of Law," pages 115–22 below.

other lawyers would do it differently, which is a good thing, and I hope some do write books of their own, differences and all.

I am speaking both to lawyers, who will naturally have their own ideas about the life of the law, and to nonlawyers, whom I hope to give a sense of how one person at least understands it. My idea is that this book can be read by students in law school and those considering it, by their teachers, by practitioners, and by people with no legal training or experience at all. This means that sometimes I will give information that is unnecessary for some readers; likewise, I will sometimes ask of the reader something that is easy for the lawyer, hard for the nonlawyer.

The book is written in two voices: the voice of the legal expositor and critic in the body of the chapters, where I mainly speak of the reader in the third person, and the voice in the passages between the chapters, where I ask questions of and invite responses from the reader, whom I here mainly address in the second person, as "you." I hope these two voices complement each other, even, and perhaps especially, where there is tension between them.

The questions I put at the end of each chapter are meant to offer topics of thought for your consideration, not to call for instant answers. You of course may have questions of your own, in which case I encourage you to write them down. Questions of both kinds, yours and mine, can be something of a guide to future reading and thinking, a kind of tool-kit with which to approach both the chapters that follow and your other experiences of law, past and future.

The idea is that as you respond to the material in the text, both as you first read it and as you respond to my questions or your own, you will be engaging with it as a lawyer might, and thus be in a better position to see what it is we may be losing.

2

It is important to say that the threat to the law I speak of is not an entirely new thing or the work of any one person or group. As I will say in chapter five, some of the movements I deplore have been at work for some time and are quite widespread.

But things do seem to be changing very fast, and it is impossible to predict where we will be when this book is actually published, let alone two or three years later. We may by then have gone in a very good direction or a very bad one, or may be in a kind of unresolved chaos or worse. My hope is that this book will contribute in a small way to the strengthening of law and democracy, or at least to the preservation of its memory.

3

The first section of the book consists of three chapters on standard legal subjects: the Model Penal Code developed by the American Law Institute, a pair of judicial opinions by Oliver Wendell Holmes, and the way the law talks—and should talk—about what we call "race," especially in the context of what is called "affirmative action."

I hope what I say about these topics is valid and useful on the merits and as a matter of legal analysis. But as presented in this book I mean these chapters to have an additional and different kind of meaning, as examples of the kind of legal thought and expression that is now in danger of being lost. They represent, that is, versions of a widely shared activity, the activity of law, that is my real subject. It is that which I hope we can keep alive.

My aim is not only to represent that activity but to stimulate it in the reader. That is, as you read these chapters I hope you find yourself responding to points I make—to lines of argument, tentative conclusions, invocations of legal experience—and doing so sometimes with approval, sometimes with doubt, sometimes in opposition. In doing these things you will be engaging in the activity of law itself, and I hope you will feel that to be important.

For readers who have a legal education and training like my own this may seem familiar, fitting a bit like an old glove; for younger lawyers, and those who are not lawyers at all, it may seem strange and awkward. But even if it does, I still hope you will articulate your views to yourself as you read and do so in ways that engage your mind and imagination. If you do, you will be learning a certain way of doing law.[2]

---

2. Over the years I have written quite a lot about what I think excellence in legal thought and writing might be, most recently in *Living Speech: Resisting the Empire of Force* (2006). I could try to summarize what I have said elsewhere, but that would be a cumbersome and unsatisfactory exercise. Instead my object here is to present examples of what I think of as

The first level of the response I hope to stimulate in you as the reader is to think about the substantive legal questions I discuss, engaging with me as a fellow lawyer, even if you are doing this for the first time. The second level of response is to think about what you are doing when you respond, positively or negatively, to what you read—for, as I say, this will be one definition of the activity of law that is my subject. As you read, that is, you will be engaging in your own version of the activity of law, and I hope as you do that you can reflect on its nature and character and value.

I also hope for a third level of response, which is that you will raise your eyes from the page and ask yourself what it means for you and for our country and its life that the questions raised here are thought about as they are in the material you read, and in your own responses to it, that is, in the way of law. This is to ask what it means that we are part of a widespread legal culture, in which myriads of similar questions are constantly being contested and thought about and resolved in something like the way displayed here.

The law that I am hoping we can keep alive is a whole way of thinking and acting with each other. It is present in every state, every city, every courthouse, every law office, making up a web of connections that provides much of the informal constitution of our country.

How does the mode of thought set forth here, in which you yourself will engage, define and shape our public life? Who are the actors here—judges, legislators, the Framers of the Constitution, lawyers—and what is the character of their relation with each other? With what degree of respect or skepticism does the good judge approach a statute, say, or contract? With what fears and hopes? Who do the human actors become when they adopt these roles? Who are we as citizens and lawyers: how are we talked about, how are we spoken to? How are these identities defined by the practices of legal thought I am trying to define?

What does it mean to live in a world like this? If it is lost, what will be lost?

---

legal excellence, which I mean to offer to you as an experience from which you can work out your own sense of it. Of course I do reveal my views, but I mean them only as suggestive. It is important to the life of this book that you engage with it in a way that makes the questions your own.

Take for example the first chapter: what does it mean to live in a world in which there is a private organization called the American Law Institute which sees its responsibility as reforming the law, and doing so with the desire to make it more intelligible, more coherent, and more just? Here the subject is the criminal law, perhaps its most important branch: what does it mean that it is talked about as it is in this Model Code? What does it mean that judges and legislators have, are really required to have, the kind of knowledge that is the subject of this chapter?

Chapter two shifts focus from legislation to judicial action, trying to explicate two opinions by Justice Holmes in such a way as to identify the nature of his extraordinary achievement. In chapter three I address the question of "affirmative action," showing how I at least would define the questions presented by this practice and how I would try to resolve them. Here in particular I am implicitly inviting you to criticize what I am doing, because in that very criticism you will be acting out of your own sense of what the law should be.

The remaining three chapters continue to address and modify these questions. They consist of a brief chapter defining the art of the law as the art of confronting and living with a certain set of tensions; a chapter outlining the threats to which I think law has been subject for some time now; and a chapter in which I define the kind of education of mind and character that I think is needed if we are to survive the present crisis of democracy and law.

I think of law and democracy together because in our country I think they are so intertwined as to be different facets of the same reality. All of our law has its roots in democratic institutions which derive their authority, directly or indirectly, from what we call "the people." On the other side, democracy works through the law, again directly or indirectly. That is the only way it can work. In a real sense we cannot have our democracy without our law, or our law without our democracy. It is in fact this combination of law and democracy that gives us our national character and identity.

This is not equally true of every democratic state. Think of France, which has its own deep culture upon which the French can base their collective identity even through periods of invasion, puppet governments, and new and different constitutions. Much the same can be said of Italy and Greece and maybe many other countries too. But for us, it is our peculiar national combination of democracy and law that makes us who we are. It is our national culture and identity.

4

This means that when our law and democracy are threatened, everything we are and care about is threatened too.

In all of this I am moved partly by something said by the journalist Sarah Kendzior, who has studied the emergence of dictatorial regimes and thinks the future of our democracy is a bleak one:

> Write down what you value; what standards you hold for yourself and for others. Write about your dreams for the future and your hopes for your children. Write about the struggle of your ancestors and how the hardships they overcame shaped the person you are today. Write your biography, write down your memories. Because if you do not do it now, you may forget.[3]

It is in this spirit that I have put together this book. I hope that it will be a record—more than a record, an experience—of some of the ways in which law could still be imagined and understood and talked about in our country at a time when we began to be aware that this could all be lost. I also hope that by the end I have suggested ways in which, even in disaster, we can still live with the law and do so in ways that will keep some of its essential quality alive.

As must be obvious, I do not mean this book to be either exclusive or exhaustive. Quite the contrary, this is just my own version of a complex institution, a set of practices, at a moment when they seem threatened. I hope others will offer their own, using their own examples. This is a collective activity. We need each other to create ways of remembering who we still are and what we still value.

What I hope comes through more than anything else is the love I have for the law that I am trying to make real for my reader. It has been a blessing to be able to spend my life doing it.

---

3. "We are Heading into Dark Times," *De Correspondent*, November 18, 1916.

Keep Law Alive

1

Legal Knowledge as an Art: Reading (and Writing) a Statute

I start with an introduction to the way the law works in the lives of lawyers and judges, asking in particular what kind of knowledge it requires and makes possible. My view is that this is knowledge not just of rules or concepts, but of an art that is essentially literary and compositional in nature. Here I will try to show how this art can work in the context of reading—and by implication of writing—a statute. The next chapter will deal with another important form of legal thought and expression, the judicial opinion.

My object in both of these chapters is to engage the reader with the way our law works when it is working well. This activity cannot be reduced to a rule book or a single set of criteria or techniques, but involves a whole-minded response on the part of legislator or judge or lawyer simultaneously to the realities of our world and to the inheritance of thought and experience expressed in what we call the materials of law—prior cases and statutes, existing understandings and expectations—including the hopes we have for a more just future. One thing that makes our law rare and precious is the way in which human minds and hearts can be engaged in its activities and processes.

My hope is that this chapter will help you form, or deepen, your own sense of what legal thinking is, and that in the process you may discover, or rediscover, some of its inherent qualities and their value.

As you read, pay attention to the questions you find yourself asking and the objections you are raising, for these are essential to the kind of engagement in legal thought I hope you experience. And think about this question as well: what does it mean that these issues are addressed in this way in our world? What kind of world does it make?

WHAT DO WE KNOW WHEN WE KNOW THE LAW? I asked a rabbi I know how he would answer that question with respect to Jewish law. Does someone know the law when he can repeat the rules that tell him what to do? Or when he can engage in the activity of reading them, separately or in conjunction with each other, and applying them sensibly to new circumstances? Is even that enough? My friend said it was not: he must know who he is in relation to the law, both as an individual and as a member of a people; this means that he must know that this law is part of a covenant with the God of Israel and he must understand the story that connects that God with this people. In particular he or she must recognize that this law was given to the Hebrew people just after their escape from slavery, at the moment when they attained the free and autonomous state that made them capable of receiving the simultaneous gift and restraint of law.[1]

Sketchy and incomplete as these remarks are, I want to take them as a model of a certain kind of legal knowledge.

What Lawyers Know

Particularly in the academic world, knowledge is now often talked about quite differently, as something objective, stateable, verifiable—out there in the world, where it can be seen and passed around, as a kind of infor-

1. In *Ever Since Sinai,* Jakob Petuchowski makes an additional point: that one must come to see the law not simply as "legislation," that is as an impersonal and abstract system of obligations, but as a "command," from one person to another, both building upon and shaping the relationship between them. Jakob Petuchowski, *Ever Since Sinai,* 78–80 (1961). One might compare Zechariah Chafee's interesting observation that a constitutional provision like the first amendment "is much more than an order to Congress not to cross the boundary which marks the extreme limits of unlawful suppression. It is also an exhortation and a guide for the action of Congress inside that boundary." Zechariah Chafee, Jr., "Freedom of Speech in War Time," 32 *Harvard Law Review* 932, 934 (1919). For a work giving striking content to the idea that the law is a gift, see Abraham Joshua Heschel, *The Sabbath* (1951).

mation. And it is often imagined not as the work of an individual mind, or group of minds, but as the product of a system or process of some kind. It is in this way objectified and reified, even commodified.

But such an image will not work for legal knowledge, which is something of a puzzle. Contrary to the stereotype nonlawyers often have of it, the law cannot be reduced to a set of rules or other propositions. Every law student who has turned to a commercial outline of one of her courses comes to recognize this, sometimes painfully, when she takes the exam and sees that the knowledge of the law on which she is being tested is not simply the capacity to repeat the rules, but something else, including at least the ability to think about them, to interpret them separately and in relation to each other, to bring them to bear—whatever that metaphor obscures—upon real and imagined events, and to do this with an eye not only to what the law is but what it should be.

As I have often found myself saying, knowledge of the law is like knowledge of a language: you never know all of it, you never know it perfectly, and you cannot reduce your knowledge of it to a set of directions or descriptions or rules; rather, your competence consists in being able to use it more or less well, in one set of situations or another. For you learn the law in order to use it—in order to achieve a set of objectives, to establish and maintain a set of relations, to move yourself and others in a direction you wish to go, even to discover that direction.

You never achieve perfect mutuality of understanding with other lawyers, with the court, or with your client, for that is always beyond us; rather, you use your ability to reduce, to define, to make more manageable the uncertainties that are present in every human situation. Legal knowledge is knowledge, but it is not an object, not restateable. It is a way of claiming meaning for experience.

Another friend of mine, an art historian and psychologist, once asked me, "What is the law's interest in truth?" His impression was that the law is a welter of confusing and competing claims, in which everyone is opposed to everyone else. He thought it was the opposite of the kind of scientific community in which people act cooperatively towards the common goal of the discovery of truth. His implication was that the law was by comparison defective, maybe even contemptible.

I think he is right that the law is not organized towards truth in the way science is, nor towards a scientific kind of truth. But I do not think that it is for this reason at all contemptible: the main goal of law is not truth, but justice, a human value of at least equal dignity and importance.[2] Justice in fact is part of the definition of law: without a commitment to defining and redefining that crucial value, law as we know it would not exist.

But this fact at once shapes and makes puzzling what we can mean by legal knowledge. It is not like scientific knowledge: not propositional, not descriptive, in nature; not primarily conceptual, or analytic, or empirical; it is not about truth, but justice. Truth has a place in the law, a crucially important place, but it is hard to see and explain what this is.

One kind of truth law has might be called constitutive: it creates a world of power and meaning, through which conflicts can be adjudicated, the habits of thought and feeling we call "norms" can be established, the government itself created and regulated. The law creates patterns of thought and imagination through which we can connect to each other over time and distance in deep ways. Think of *Brown v. Board of Education,* which was not only just, but true.

It is especially difficult to understand the place of truth in law in light of the fact that we structure legal conversations about justice in part through the form of a contest, or what we call the adversary system. It is not the only way to do it, but it is our way, and it has the implication that what we say is always in principle contestable. Any claim that the law is this or that, or should be read in this or that way, must be made with the awareness that someone else, with adverse interests, may challenge it. In a case of sufficient magnitude, anything that can rationally be contested will be contested.

The law is thus a way of constantly testing the limits of what can be said, what can be claimed, in our legal language. The effect is to create an odd double sense: first, that everything is in principle up for grabs, uncertain, unstable; and, on the other hand, that what is unchallenged—what the lawyers share—is remarkably firm, for even these bright and asser-

2. To avoid misunderstanding, perhaps I need to say that I do not mean that law has no regard for truth in the usual sense. Obviously it does, not only in the trial of factual issues but in the identification and interpretation of authoritative texts. Rather, my point is that its goal or end, what Aristotle would call its *telos,* is not to arrive at a true account of the world, as is the case with science, but at a judgment or rule that will be just—and for that to happen it must be based on truth of the kinds I have mentioned here and in the text. Certainly the trial judge wants a case to be decided on the basis of the truth, and does what she can to be sure that happens. In a complex but real way the trial is itself a search for truth.

tive people, with every interest in challenging it, are finding that they cannot reasonably do so.

Disagreement in the law is thus a way of establishing and confirming agreement, and that is a form of truth. This is so not only in connection with the formal argument of cases but also in negotiation, where lawyers regularly come to rough agreement as to what the law means and requires. To carry on this double-edged conversation one must have an important kind of knowledge, knowledge of what can and cannot be said. It is a kind of cultural knowledge.

But just as disagreement establishes what is agreed upon, one function of agreement is to define disagreement. It is our agreement about almost all the material available to us as lawyers in a particular case—say, the identity and meaning of the relevant statutes and judicial opinions and administrative judgments—that enables us to define our disagreement in a useful way, to make it intelligible and amenable to resolution; beyond that, it may lead us to the discovery of possibilities we had not contemplated. In law, as in science, knowledge thus has the function of focusing our attention on what we do not know—though what we mean by knowledge and ignorance in the two cases is different.

Thus, I want to begin by saying that law is not a body of knowledge that can be reduced to propositions or rules. Its primary goal is not scientific truth—though it has its own commitments to other sorts of truth—but justice. Legal knowledge is an activity of mind, a way of doing something with the rules and cases and other materials of law, an activity that is itself not reducible to a set of directions or any fixed description. It is a species of cultural competence, like learning a language; this may in fact be the closest analogy we have, for what a lawyer knows at the center is how to speak and write the language of the law, in actual situations in the world—how to use legal language to create legal meaning. Legal knowledge is in the end not merely conceptual or factual but rhetorical and imaginative.

The Lawyer as Writer

Of course the lawyer must in some sense know the rules and understand the conceptual relations they express or establish, complex as they may be, and she must be able to move with confidence into other fields, from history to technology, and be ready to learn facts of all kinds—historical, technical, scientific, and so on. But all of that knowledge, important as it is, is really the material upon which her other knowledge works, as she figures out what it is possible for her to say, and how best to say it. The lawyer's knowledge is a writer's knowledge.

The lawyer is a special kind of writer, with her own particular relations both to the language she uses and to the people she addresses. She is an advocate and an adviser, acting always in the interest of another, and she uses the language of the law, and her ability as a writer, to advance the welfare of her client. Does this mean that her use of language is inherently instrumental in nature—a tool to achieve objectives she does not state, for motives she does not reveal? Or can it have an essential quality of sincerity or authenticity?

Sometimes, of course, the lawyer's speech and writing look wholly instrumental: in arguing a close point about jurisdiction or conflicts of laws, for example, the lawyer is not expressing what the client really believes or wants or understands. She is using this language to attain a result. But even here there is a sense in which she has to mean what she says, or her argument is false, and will likely be seen to be.

She need not mean that she would decide the case the way she is arguing, if she were the judge; but she must mean that the argument she makes is a respectable one, the best that can be made on behalf of her client in fact, and that the judge could decently and honorably rest upon it. And "best" not only in the sense that it is the argument most likely to prevail; she is saying that this is the best formulation of her client's case that can be made in our legal language—the one that best serves the most fundamental purposes of law, most fully respects the decisions made by others (legislatures, judges, agencies, private persons) that bear upon the case, and most accurately identifies and interprets the texts that govern it. She is making the best case for her client that the materials of law permit, and the "best" as seen not only from her client's point of view but also from that of the law.[3]

Of course lots of lawyers do not in this sense mean what they say, but I think this costs them and their clients a great deal, for the people they address will often at some level recognize this fact and discount what they hear. The kind of lawyer who will obviously say anything that she

3. For a fuller statement of this position, see *Heracles' Bow*, 215–37 (1985).

thinks will help her client—and there are plenty of them—will not be listened to by sensible judges.

But there are lawyers who regularly command the respect and trust of their audience—their judges actually want to hear what they have to say—and my impression is that this mainly happens when their audience is confident that the lawyer is speaking to them, in the special sense in which I mean the term, sincerely, that is, out of a kind of truth. While there is one sense, then, in which the lawyer's use of language is instrumental, her motives ulterior, there is another sense in which she can and should mean what she says. In fact, a crucial part of legal knowledge is knowing how to mean what you say in the language of the law.

Legal knowledge is thus constantly created and recreated, differently by different minds on different occasions. We say that any good lawyer would know that a certain case or statute bore upon the case before him, and would make, in a general way, some of the same arguments—for want of jurisdiction over the person, for example, or for the application of Illinois law. But we also know that these arguments would be made in very different ways by different lawyers, even—or especially—by very good lawyers, and that it is in these differences that many of the most important qualities of professional and intellectual excellence can be discerned. An essential part of legal knowledge is invention.

Not only invention: criticism, for in using legal language the lawyer must be ready to subject it to critical judgment, from the outside as well as the inside, and to propose, or perform, transformations of it. A convention that drives this process in our world, really makes it possible, is the principle of legal argument that the lawyer must show that the result for which he argues is compelled both by the law, as he defines and redefines it, and by justice. To admit either that the result for which one argues is unjust, though compelled by the law, or that it is not warranted by the law, though it is just, would in our system be fatal—and fatal in a judicial opinion as well as in an argument.

Suppose for example that you are trying to enforce a contractual penalty for nonperformance, which the other side says is too severe to be enforced. You will argue not only that the penalty is permissible under relevant case and statutory law, but that the rule validating it is a just one: it respects the free choices of the contracting parties; it tends to produce efficient results because it encourages the bargained allocation of risk; it makes possible certain high-risk investments by placing the loss on the party whose anticipated benefits are typically highest; and so forth. The lawyer on the other side will maintain not only that a penalty in excess of actual damages is unjust, but that the relevant case and statutory law, properly interpreted, prohibit it at least in this egregious form. And a judge too will struggle to show not only that the penalty is valid or invalid under existing law, but that the law as he reads it is fair and sensible and proper.

Of course there will be argument about what "justice" means in a particular case, just as there will be about the "law" that bears upon it. And I do not mean that there is or should be one single conception of justice to which all lawyers appeal. My point is that the structure of a legal argument is in a serious way imperfect or incomplete if it does not include the topic of justice as well as that of law.

In our arguments, then, the result must be justified by law *and* justice. We are in this sense both positivists and natural lawyers at the same time. The effect of this principle is to subject law itself to constant pressure and criticism. The lawyer must always be prepared to ask where the law itself has gone wrong, what voices or claims or understandings it improperly excludes or admits. Our law is capable of great evil, and the lawyer must be ready to see how that is so; ready, that is, to reimagine if necessary both the world and the law.

How does all this work?

One place to start is with the moment at which the lawyer's mind meets the language she is required to use—the language of the law—and with a set of questions about that language. What is this language like? What does it leave out, distort, or exclude? What does it enable her to do, and what does it inhibit or prevent? When we have some sense of possible answers to these questions, we can begin to ask the next one: By what art is this language used well, that is, with both practical and ethical success? What does it mean to "know" the language of a particular field of law, to understand and to be able to use its rules, principles, cases, and other materials?

The Model Penal Code

As my first instance of legal knowledge I want to look at the criminal law, which has been the object of especially intelligent and thoroughgoing efforts at reform and integration. I shall of necessity be rather brief, but I think that it may be helpful to take even a superficial look at the language of a whole field, asking what opportunities and difficulties it creates for the lawyer or judge—or legislator—who tries to speak in the ways it makes possible.

Codifying the Criminal Law

The effort of reform I speak of received its fullest and most influential expression a half century ago in the Model Penal Code, which has since helped shape statutory reform in almost every state.

The goal of the Code was to offer a method of thought, both for the drafters and for the readers of criminal statutes, that would transform the confused and contradictory field of criminal law into a coherent system. At its center is the idea of blameworthiness or culpability, which is used both to determine criminality itself and to assess its degree. Blameworthiness in turn is conceived of as a function of intentionality or state of mind, and here the Code made an important advance. Instead of simply asking the crude question of much of prior law—whether the defendant had a "guilty" or "bad" mind (*mens rea*), as a kind of raw moral judgment—the Code engages in a much more refined process. It first identifies each of the material elements of the offense—in a hypothetical crime of home invasion, say, "breaking and entering" a "dwelling house" in the "nighttime"—then assigns one of four different states of mind (or degrees of culpability) to each of the elements: purpose, knowledge, recklessness, or negligence.[4]

The idea of the Code is that the legislative assignment of degrees of culpability to the different elements is to be the product of a reasoned judgment, based upon the fundamental principle that the criminal law should provide a graduated set of punishments to reflect graduated lev-

4. Thus the Code might require in the hypothetical case "knowledge" that the building is a dwelling house, but "negligence" with respect to the time, on the ground that the former element is more important to the assessment of the culpability of the action and actor. If so, a conviction could only be obtained if the prosecution proved that the defendant actually knew the building was a dwelling house, but it need show only that the defendant should have known that it was nighttime. For definitions of the degrees of culpability, see *Model Penal Code* § 2.02 (1962).

Earlier law drew rather rough distinctions with respect to state of mind partly because it drew rather rough distinctions in the definition of crimes and punishments as well. At common law, the main question of grading was whether the defendant committed a felony

els of blameworthiness. This is the way in which the purposes of the criminal law can rationally be attained.[5] Of course, in all of this the Code is not writing on a clean slate, as a total innovation, but trying to draw on the best of the preexisting tradition.

Interpretation

As I suggest above, the Code implicitly provides a method not only for the drafting of statutes but also for their interpretation; one can take a statute drafted in the old days, in much cruder terms—speaking, say, of "willfulness" or "unlawfulness" or "wantonness"—and say that the real question to be asked by lawyers and judges is what degree of culpability (as defined by the Code) the statute should be construed to require with respect to each of its material elements.

Its method is thus in important respects transformational, for it provides a language of greater refinement and complexity into which conversations traditionally couched in other terms can usefully be translated. For example, consider the standard common law doctrine that a "mistake of fact" is no defense to a "general intent" crime, but may be a defense to a "special intent" crime, while "mistake of law" is never a defense. In the textbook case of *State v. Woods*[6]—where a woman charged

---

(for which death and forfeiture were the usual penalties) or only a misdemeanor. For these purposes a rather basic language of "guilty mind" (*mens rea*), "bad motive," "wickedness," and so forth might be thought to work well enough. The Code's fine elaboration of degrees of culpability is thus directly related to its effort to grade crimes carefully according to blameworthiness.

5. Traditionally, criminal law is conceived to have four purposes: deterrence, restraint, rehabilitation, and retribution. The Model Penal Code rejected retribution as a proper goal and added several others, among them: to protect conduct that is without fault from condemnation as criminal; to give fair warning of criminal prohibitions; to safeguard against excessive, disproportionate, or arbitrary punishment; to coordinate and harmonize the duties of courts and administrative agencies dealing with crime and offenders; and to advance the use of scientific methods in the sentencing and treatment of offenders. *See id.* § 1.02. The Code has of course been criticized, especially for its attempted elimination of retribution, which some consider the foundation of criminal law, especially since the Code's central concept of culpability seems to suggest a measure of responsibility based upon desert. For a helpful treatment of the purposes of punishment, see Kent Greenawalt, "Punishment," in 4 *Encyclopedia of Crime and Justice* 1336 (Sanford H. Kadish ed., 1983), as well as the collection of materials in Sanford H. Kadish & Stephen J. Schulhofer, *Criminal Law and Its Processes* 113–85 (5th ed., 1989).

6. 179 Atlantic Reporter 1 (Vt. 1935).

with sleeping with "another woman's husband" raised as a defense that she (as it turns out erroneously) believed the man to have had a valid divorce—the Vermont court approached the question by asking whether the concededly good faith mistake was one of "law" or "fact."[7]

But in this context these words are virtually empty terms of conclusion; what should shape the conversation is the question whether it is a wise reading of this language to punish this woman, and people similarly situated, under this statute, given the language and purpose of the statute and the purposes of the criminal law more generally. This is exactly the consequence of the Code's method, which asks what degree of culpability this statute should be read to require with respect to the central element, "another woman's husband." Should she be punished only if she actually knew she was sleeping with someone validly married to another, or should it be enough that she was reckless or negligent with respect to this circumstance? Or should it be the case, as the Vermont court actually held, that she should be punished even if she was wholly innocent of the fact that he was still married to another?[8] To frame the question this way directs attention away from an empty clash of conclusions to the language and policy of the statute and to the purposes of criminal punishment itself.

Or consider a statute that defines rape as "sexual intercourse by a man with a woman against her will." The defendant admits sexual intercourse, but claims he believed that the woman was consenting; she says that she was not, and that his contrary belief was unreasonable. Under prior law, it was usual to ask whether the statute should be read to imply an unstated requirement of *mens rea,* or a "guilty mind," with respect to her nonconsent; if so, it would require for conviction that he actually knew that she was not consenting; if the statute were not read that way, he would be guilty of rape even if his belief in her consent was honest and reasonable.

The Model Penal Code offers two intermediate alternatives, "negligence" and "recklessness": under the first, the defendant can be guilty of rape if his good faith belief is unreasonable; under the second, he can

---

7. *See id.* at 2–3.

8. *See id.* at 3. On the merits of this question, the Code would preclude the last possibility—that she should be punished even if she were without fault as to this material element of the offense—under the principles of section 2.02(1).

be guilty if he recognizes and consciously disregards the risk that she is not consenting.

The Code is thus telling legislatures to choose the degree of culpability explicitly, for each of the elements, and to assign punishments that are proportional to the blameworthiness so defined. Although it does not say so outright, in effect it also tells judges and lawyers who are facing a statute which does not explicitly assign degrees of culpability, as the Code does, that the question of culpability is still present for each of the elements, and should be decided on a principled basis.

In every case the issue is what degree of culpability the statute in question should be read to require with respect to each of its material elements. This all adds up to what might be called a discourse, a rhetoric, or, as I prefer to say, a language: a set of topics and materials for thought and argument. As we have seen in *State v. Woods*, the lawyer now has something to say about the cases that come to her that she would not have if the Code did not exist. The Code is an effort to make the whole of criminal law coherent and just, and to this end it invites arguments by the lawyers, and reflection by the judge, of a more complex and reasoned sort than was encouraged or made possible by prior law.

Putting the Code to Work

If this will do as a sketch of the aims and structure of the Model Penal Code, we can now ask: what would it be like to try to use this language as lawyer or judge, to try to put it to work as the material of thought? Or, to speak in terms of my title: what kind of legal knowledge does it create, require, and make possible in those who use it?

The first step in learning this language would be to try to understand the purposes the Code is trying to serve and its basic method for doing so, as I have described them above, putting aside for the moment its particular rules. What we need most to understand, that is, is the way the Code imagines itself, and the world, and what it is trying to do.

The Code's self-conception—in this it is a little like the law of which my friend the rabbi was speaking—is reflected in a story of a certain kind, which itself runs like this. The world of the criminal law before the Code was a morass of confusion and contradiction, disorganization, and ignorance, all amounting to serious injustice unworthy of an enlightened state. The Code applied careful, sustained, and collective thought to render this body of law coherent, orderly, and just—and just, not only in the sense that the law is predictable, that results in like cases are similar, and so forth, but in a more substantive sense, for all this is achieved in the name of a coherent and sensible set of purposes that are themselves shaped by a ruling conception of justice, based upon principles of culpability.

Like all legislation, the Code is in a sense incomplete, for it is not self-executing; but as we have seen it does give directions to its own use, which are meant to enable lawyers and judges to use it rationally and coherently. Unlike the law of which the rabbi spoke, the Code is not a gift to the people upon their becoming free, but it is deeply related to human freedom nonetheless, for it is itself an exercise of freedom and reason, an effort to function wisely and well. More than that: its definition of the occasions on which freedom may be taken from a citizen is also a definition of freedom, a definition meant to be a just one. Such is the promise of the Code, and it is to a remarkable extent realized.

Conflicts of Discourse and of Purpose

But it is not surprising for a lawyer to learn that in practice things do not entirely work out in this orderly and coherent way. To start with, the lawyer would quickly see that she had to master not just one discourse, that of the Code, but two others with which it is often in tension: the prior criminal law, which the Code was intended to reform (both for the points at which the Code differs from it and for the continuing assumptions that connect the two bodies of thought); and a more general language of goal and limit, philosophical in kind, since nearly every case can be the occasion for asking what the proper goals of the criminal law should be and what limits should be placed upon it—and sometimes as an explicitly constitutional matter.[9]

The Code must be read, that is, as poised between two other systems of discourse with which it is, potentially at least, always in tension.

In addition, there are conflicts internal to the Code, most notably among the purposes of the criminal law upon which the Code relies for its claims to coherence, and these present obvious difficulties for anyone trying to use it. The Code assumes that its main purposes—restraint, deterrence, and rehabilitation—are harmonious or, if they do conflict

9. For an important example, see *Powell v. Texas*, 392 U.S. 514 (1968).

in a particular case, that they permit a kind of trade-off, of one "good" for another.

But none of the purposes is itself entirely coherent, and there are severe tensions among them. There is, for example, in the idea of restraint alone no principle of limit—one could restrain forever anyone who presented any threat of criminality, except for other considerations of fairness and utility not implicit in the term itself. Much the same can be said about deterrence, for it is hard to see how, simply in terms of deterrence alone, there can be too much or too frequent punishment.

Responsible thought thus requires the consideration of other and incompatible values. Rehabilitation does have the inherent limit that one will stop punishment when the cure has occurred, but this is difficult in the extreme to assess and may lead to releases that are too early, or too late, when measured by other values, such as the seriousness of the offense. As for retribution—a traditional purpose of the criminal law not accepted by the Code—it is usually supposed to have an implicit and beneficent limit, though I think in fact people typically want more than an eye for an eye. And in any event, by what scale is one to say that such and such a term in prison is an act of retribution "proportionate" to an arson attempt, say, or a physical assault or filing a false tax return?

The Code seems to assume that what we call trade-offs can occur among these various purposes, but it does not tell us what trade-offs are to be made, nor is it clear that they can in fact be made in a rational and satisfactory manner. How does one decide how much deterrence or rehabilitation to insist on, or to give up? The goals are not simply competing desiderata, but are often in true opposition with each other.

This is especially true of rehabilitation and deterrence, for these forms of punishment imply radically different relations between the state and the individual, between which no compromise is possible. One kind of punishment treats him as an end in himself, the other treats him simply as a means for the effectuation of social policy, and you cannot say simultaneously that you care about another person and that you do not.[10]

There is also an even more basic question: whether the practice of punishment can ever be rationally shaped to any set of stateable purposes in the way the Code assumes it can. It may be, that is, that punishment is

10. For an elaboration of the incoherence this conflict creates, see *Heracles' Bow,* 192–214.

an activity that human communities have always engaged in for motives that cannot be wholly articulated or even completely understood, and that the kind of rationalization the Code attempts creates an intolerable fiction. One might well doubt, for example, whether it is possible to eliminate the retributive element from punishment by simply saying so, as the Code attempts to do. The lawyer or judge using the Code must accordingly be always ready to ask how—on what understandings, with what qualifications—it is possible to use, in a sensible way, a language that purports to shape the criminal law by reference to what it declares to be its purposes, when that effort must always be to some degree fictional.

One might have similar doubts about whether the Code's fundamental idea—that one can precisely determine blameworthiness by making fine judgments of states of mind, or degrees of culpability, with respect to the various elements of an offense—really works. Is this something juries or judges or lawyers can actually do? Or are we actually better off with vaguer terms like "willful" and "wrongful," which leave to the trier of fact a larger question of net moral evaluation?[11]

Finally, and perhaps most tellingly, there is a deep tension between the rational and enlightened way the Code tries to make the trial of guilt proceed and the way the other stages of the criminal process work.

Think for example of the police officer's decision to arrest, the pros-

---

11. Consider also the tension inherent in the claim that the criminal trial should focus exclusively on what the defendant *did*, leaving the larger question, who the defendant *is*, for determination at the sentencing hearing. This is an artificial distinction: jury members naturally want to know as much as they can about the defendant's character and history, and the lawyers, when it is to their advantage to do so, struggle to tell them. Sometimes—as in deciding whether a killing is "provoked" and therefore manslaughter, or with "malice" and therefore murder, or "premeditated" and therefore murder in the first degree—it is virtually impossible to separate the two kinds of question.

Similarly, the basic conception of the human actor at work in the criminal law is not wholly coherent, and the Code cannot make it so. Most of the time the law assumes that the individual is a free and autonomous actor, responsible for his conduct and its consequences. Defenses are fashioned to remove from liability those who are thought not to be in control of their lives—the insane, the sleepwalking, and the like. But the truth is much muddier than this suggests: we are all the products of circumstance; no one is entirely free; yet almost all of us have a residue of autonomy and hence responsibility. Neither of the two extreme images of human freedom is entirely valid, but the law has great difficulty reflecting this fact. What this means for the user of this language, whether lawyer or judge, is that she tends to vacillate uncomfortably between two incompatible and impossible positions, without any way of saying what she may believe to be true about human freedom and determinism. For a

ecutor's judgment whether to indict or to accept a plea bargain, the judge's sentencing decision (itself often based on a report made by the probation department), and the parole board's decision to release or restrain—none of these judgments is or should be reducible to the clear-cut forms of argument described above. This is not a matter of intellectual incoherence only: there is a profound and disturbing conflict between the rationality and idealism of the Code's method for determining who should be punished and the often hideous realities of criminal law in practice, especially the brutality of punishment itself as often inflicted in our country.[12] The shouting chasm between the pretenses of the law and its reality is of course much worse when race and class are taken into account.

Facing Tensions and Contradictions

Thus it is that when we try to understand the motives and premises of the Code, what it is trying to do with prior law, its conception of culpability or blameworthiness, its effort to render a mass of contradictory and confusing material understandable, all so that we can read with intelligence the provisions of the Code itself and use them sensibly in thought and argument—so that we can become, that is, speakers as well as readers of this language—we discover that the Code falls very far short of the coherence at which it aims.

As I have suggested it is riven with unavoidable and unresolvable tensions and contradictions, which go to the very center of its way of imagining the defendant, the trier of fact, and the process of punishment itself—and I am sure there are more than I have listed. One who

---

valuable treatment of this issue, see Thomas A. Green, *Freedom and Criminal Responsibility in American Legal Thought* (2014).

12. Rehabilitation is not, as far as I can see, in any real sense the object of our penitentiaries; restraint is, but it is usually temporary, and the convicts are often treated in ways that make it more likely, not less, that they will commit crimes in the future. Retribution is perhaps achieved, but it is often brutal, uncivilized, and costly; deterrence may or may not be much achieved by this system—one certainly doubts whether it is achieved to a higher degree than it would be by a humane or civilized system of penology. We have both an astonishingly high percentage of our population in prison and an astonishingly high rate of crime and recidivism. On the other hand, it is important to say that the idealism of the Code can be seen as essential to its achievement, which is to refine and elevate our discourse by holding out a higher standard of rationality and decency than we can normally attain and thus to make possible an effective criticism of what we do.

wishes to master this language, then, and to use it effectively, must understand it not simply as a logical system but must learn how to live with its particular incoherencies, its splits and breakdowns. One kind of legal knowledge it requires, then, is a capacity to face and manage its internal contradictions and tensions.

Although I cannot prove it, I think that what is true of the Model Penal Code would be true, in different ways and degrees, of any attempt to produce a comprehensive and coherent code regulating a field of law. To the extent I am right, the capacity that I say the Code calls upon in its user—a capacity to use a language despite its incoherences, to recognize what it omits or distorts—is an essential part of legal knowledge more generally.

What attitude should we take towards the tensions and fissures within the Code? One possibility is to deplore them as proofs of failure, even to give up on it all as a sham or façade. But this I think is to yield too readily to disappointment and frustration; one can see these aspects of the Code more benignly, as defining over and over again, and thus making available to argument and thought, the most profound and disturbing questions about the nature of punishment and the structure of our society.

It is far better that these tensions and contradictions be recognized, made overt, and thus become the object of shared concern and distress, than the most obvious alternatives, which are to bury them in language too opaque to work in this way or to insist against the facts upon the fairness and rationality of our system of criminal law.

For there are good reasons why the Code is marked by tension and contradiction, namely that the questions it addresses simply cannot be rationalized into a perfect system or order. The conflicts exist in the material and in our minds, not just in the language of the Code. In a real sense, the failures of the Code are noble ones. Like other efforts at producing knowledge, a central part of the achievement of the Code lies in its definitions of what we do not "know"—and "know" not in a purely conceptual or factual or analytic way, but in the far more important sense in which I have been using "knowledge" throughout this chapter, as a form and ground of action. The Code helps us see what we do not know how to say, or to do.

To return to my beginning point, knowledge of the criminal law is not reducible to knowledge of the rules, or even the principles, of the Model Penal Code or of a statute based upon it. It requires us to know how to use this language, and the other languages with which it is connected, including those of common law crimes and of the Constitution, and how to use them not only when they seem to work as designed but when they break down, collapsing into tension and contradiction.

The Code is itself a masterly achievement of what I am calling "writing," but in the nature of things it cannot complete its task unaided. The knowledge it requires in those who use it is not merely skill at interpretation, as that term is usually meant, but the knowledge of an art, an art of writing: a way of resisting what looks like entropy, as system after system, text after text, reveals incoherences that cannot be rationalized away. It obviously cannot be taught or learned in a mechanical or routine way, but calls upon capacities of invention and imagination. This is the kind of knowledge—a writer's knowledge—that the Code calls upon us to have.

I think it would be a good thing if all of us, as lawyers and judges and citizens, could combine, as the Code does, a fundamental commitment to a reasoned and decent vision of justice with a realistic recognition of the circumstances and values and perceptions that render it less than wholly practicable and coherent. This kind of maturity of judgment is I think a characteristic of lawyers at their best, a way of recognizing the periphery but speaking from and to the center.

As you think about the kind of criminal law the Model Penal Code is trying to create here, based upon careful judgments of blameworthiness which are in turn to be determined by states of mind, you might ask yourself how else criminal law might be imagined. As a system based on retribution for wrongful acts? As system for social control based upon estimates of the dangerousness of certain people?

What does it mean that we have the way of thinking the Code has defined? If you were to make a criminal code of your own, where would you begin? Or to shift to another situation, what advice would you give a person who was setting out to draft a statute on another topic—say immigration or divorce or progressive taxation?

What does it mean, as I asked earlier, that we have in our world the American Law Institute, a private professional organization with con-

siderable prestige but without any standing in our government, certainly without legislative power—an institution that is committed to thinking through one area of the law after another and producing at the end model codes like the one discussed above, along with what it calls "restatements" of the law, that is, reasoned summaries of what the law has been, with proposals for modification as well?

When you think again of the kind of knowledge of the law that is defined by the rabbi in the passage at the beginning of this chapter—knowledge that is in part knowing who you are, in what community and culture and context, with what history, and what shared hopes—can you recognize this kind of knowledge, or its beginnings, in yourself, as you think about the Model Penal Code and your positive or negative responses to it? Am I right that this knowledge is at bottom the knowledge of a language and how to use it?

The Model Penal Code is of course imperfect: it cannot harmonize the purposes of criminal law, nor can it regulate the processes of arrest and search and the prosecutorial judgment about what charge to bring, nor can it govern the prisons to which convicted persons are often sent, nor can it create a consistent and coherent relation either to prior criminal law or constitutional law—and you can probably think of other defects as well. What does it mean, then, that these defects continue to exist? Could you imagine getting rid of them? Do you have some sense of the way in which they can be responsibly lived with? Think here about what might be meant by what I called maturity of judgment.

Finally, do you see how it is that justice is a necessary theme in all responsible legal work in our culture? Could you imagine a criminal law code, or larger legal culture, in which that was not true?

2

Legal Knowledge as an Art: Reading (and Writing) a Judicial Opinion

Here I continue to pursue the idea of legal knowledge as an art, but do so in a new context, where the issue is not how to read, and write—and respond to—a statute, but how to read, and write—and respond to—a judicial opinion, which must itself read and respond to statutes, constitutional provisions, earlier judicial decisions, traditional assumptions, and diverse conceptions of our own national history and identity.

If the statute represents the way law is made for the future, in the form of rules and directions to conduct, the judicial opinion represents the way law is made for the present, in its effort to explain and justify a decision that resolves a particular dispute that has its roots in the past—maybe recent past, but past. The opinion also speaks to the future, of course, but less in the form of codified rules than in exemplifying a process of judgment that can itself be judged, for good or ill.

As with the statute, what is called for in the opinion is an art, not only of expression but of judgment. This art requires the engagement of the human mind and heart, the action of intelligence and imagination, together with a real aspiration to achieve justice, all in circumstances where one must understand and respond to other judgments made by other people. My hope here is to show how that art can be well performed, at least in the two opinions we read.

As you read, ask yourself what it means to our country and our culture that we have the institution of the judicial opinion.

You will see that I greatly admire the work that Justice Holmes does in the two opinions discussed here, but I don't want to create the impression that I have a high opinion of everything he does. As a lawyer would say, the issue at the moment is the quality of these two opinions, not his whole body of work.

FOR MY NEXT EXAMPLE OF LEGAL KNOWLEDGE, I turn from the remarkable challenges and opportunities presented to the writing mind by the Model Penal Code to a legal moment quite different in kind: the movement from Justice Holmes's opinion for the Court in *Schenck v. United States*[1] to his dissenting opinion in *Abrams v. United States*.[2] These were two of the first cases decided by the Supreme Court dealing with the first amendment,[3] both deservedly famous. Holmes's opinion in *Abrams* is an achievement of real significance, the beginning in fact of modern first amendment jurisprudence.

Yet I hope that the Model Penal Code will still be relevant, in that it may help us see both of these cases, as the Court initially saw them, in terms of the criminal law. This will give the reader an opportunity to put to work what he or she has just learned about the criminal law, and in that respect engage in the kind of legal thinking and expression I am trying to help keep alive.

I also mean to suggest something more general by the juxtaposition of Code and opinion, namely that the kind of striking accomplishment

1. 249 U.S. 47 (1919).

2. 250 U.S. 616 (1919).

3. The most important predecessor to these two cases was *Patterson v. Colorado*, 205 U.S. 454 (1907), in which Justice Holmes plainly suggested that the effect of the first amendment was only to outlaw prior restraints and prohibitions on speech. *Id.* at 462. This was an idea of some currency, tracing its roots to Blackstone's statement of the principle of freedom of speech in English law. On this view, speech once uttered could be punished if it fell within certain established classes of torts or crimes or was otherwise inimical to the public good, just as other conduct could be. But to say that the Supreme Court had not spoken before *Patterson* does not mean that there had been no debate and no law on freedom of speech in other institutional contexts. For the fullest and most helpful account of the first amendment before *Schenck* and *Abrams*, see David Raban, *Free Speech in Its Forgotten Years*, 285–98, 342–71 (1997).

achieved by Holmes can mark possibilities for the imaginative lawyer elsewhere in the law, perhaps even in what may seem to be the most ordinary cases, such as those involving minor crimes.

Schenck v. United States

The provision of the Espionage Act of 1917 at issue in *Schenck* made it criminal "willfully . . . to obstruct the recruiting and enlistment service of the United States," or to conspire to do so.[4] The defendants in that case sent circulars to men who had been called for the draft, denouncing the draft itself as a violation of the thirteenth amendment and the war as a design to enrich the capitalist class, but containing little if any language that could be construed as explicit advice or encouragement to refuse the draft.

Today we would see this case as presenting serious first amendment issues, but in 1918, when there was little or no first amendment jurisprudence to rely on, it was natural for the Court to see it simply as a criminal law matter. If we looked at it that way, and in pre-Code terms, the two main statutory questions would be whether the object of the conspiracy amounted to an "obstruction" and whether the defendants could be found to have the quality of intention (or guilty mind) indicated by the word "willfully."

On the first point, it is true that the defendants did not plan to interfere physically with the draft—for example by blocking the door of the receiving station with a truck—but if the recruits were persuaded by the defendants' publications, and refused the draft, that would certainly seem to be an interference that might well fall under the term "obstruction."

Should it matter that such an obstruction would depend upon an act of will by another person, the recruit who decided to refuse? The prosecution would say surely not: one who persuades or encourages another to commit a crime is under ordinary principles of law responsible as an accessory if the crime takes place. There is no notion in the criminal law, they would argue, that such a voluntary act by one party excuses

4. *Schenck v. United States*, 249 U.S. at 49 (citing the Espionage Act of June 15, 1917, ch. 30, § 3, 40 Stat. 217–219).

another who encourages the crime. It was in this sense consistent with common understandings for the Court to classify what the defendants were trying to achieve as a form of "obstruction" within the meaning of the statute.

Writing for the Court, Holmes does not explicitly define the quality of mind or intention required by the word "willfully," but he understandably has rather little difficulty finding the requirement met in this case: "Of course the document would not have been sent unless it had been intended to have some effect, and we do not see what effect it could be expected to have upon persons subject to the draft except to influence them to obstruct the carrying of it out."[5]

Once the Justices started thinking of the case in such criminal law terms, it was natural for them simply not to regard the first amendment as fairly present at all, on the ground, obvious to them, that the first amendment does not protect criminal speech, which this so plainly seemed to be. Criminal ends can be obtained by verbal as well as nonverbal means, and it would be an odd reading of the first amendment that saw such conduct as protected against punishment simply because words were chosen as the instruments of crime. Perhaps refusing induction should not be a crime; but, so long as it is, the Justices might think, it should be criminal for one person to persuade another to commit that crime, just as it would be if the crime were murder, say of a foreign dignitary or a commercial rival. To the Justices this would all seem obvious.

For Holmes, then, and the rest of the Court, the case was easy enough. The criminal law seemed to say all that needed to be said, and the defendants' invocation of the first amendment was understandably unsuccessful.

On the other hand, Holmes did respond to the first amendment argument raised by counsel and in doing so took the first steps, almost without knowing it, in the direction of an enormously influential way of thinking about the central puzzle presented by this and similar cases: ought the first amendment protect conduct, otherwise criminal, simply because it takes the form of speech? Why? And, whatever the rule is, should it protect some forms of speech more than others—the kind of

5. *Id.* at 51.

political speech involved here, for example, but not the speech necessary to maintain a numbers racket or an extortion ring?

To begin with the last point, Holmes does not address the question explicitly, but he does seem to see this kind of speech as somehow different from speech of other kinds—he says that some of the strongest expressions came from "well-known public men" and that if the defendants had been speaking in peacetime they might well have been within their "constitutional rights."[6] That he cannot fully articulate a standard of judgment is hardly surprising, since his opinion is something of a first effort to think about the kind of speech the first amendment should be read to protect.

The more fundamental question is whether speech, or some forms of speech, should enjoy a protection under the first amendment that is not available to other forms of conduct. Again, Holmes is not explicit on the point. It is not entirely clear, to me at least, whether in the quotation that follows below he means the "clear and present danger" test to establish a new constitutional rule for the protection of speech or simply to explain the principle of criminal law under which this conduct is properly punishable:

> The question in every case is whether the words used are used in such circumstances and are of such a nature as to create a clear and present danger that they will bring about the substantive evils that Congress has a right to prevent.[7]

Holmes uses this language to explain why this speech can be reached in this wartime context, when in peacetime it might be innocuous, but his point would be equally relevant whether he is thinking in constitutional or criminal law terms.

It was almost inevitable for the Justices to see *Schenck* the way they

6. *Id.* at 51–52.

7. *Id. at 52.* Although *Schenck* is formally a conspiracy case, of which the gravamen is agreement, Holmes seems to be thinking about it as an attempt case, where the question is "how close" the conduct came to inflicting the harm the defendant intended. Or he may be asking whether the means chosen to attain the goals of the conspiracy were so ill-adapted to the purpose that they presented no danger to the public. Standard classroom examples include things like conspiring to murder a foreign dignitary through magic charms or attempting to shoot down a passenger plane with a child's bow and arrow.

did, and not only because of their conservative and class-based hostility to the doctrines and persons of the defendants. The criminal law seemed adequate to deal with the case, particularly as it was pre-Code law, which drew fewer fine distinctions and rested far more confidently on net jury judgments of guilt and innocence.

Any thought about the possible bearing of the first amendment had in a sense to be conjectural, for its language had been given no effective meaning. Holmes does mention the first amendment, though only to dismiss it; yet almost without knowing it he begins to provide material for thought about it—in his talk about the wartime context, in his recognition that there is a constitutional right to carry on some sorts of as yet undesignated speech, and in his articulation of the standards of proximity and degree that the first amendment might require the criminal law to follow.

Abrams v. United States

When *Abrams v. United States*[8] was presented for decision later the same year, on generally similar facts but under a more repressive set of statutes, it is not surprising to find the Court, through Justice Clarke, affirming *Schenck* in every respect, saying simply that it had there sufficiently discussed and negated any first amendment claim.

The facts are familiar: the defendants, all Russians by birth, were distressed by the American invasion of Russia in 1918 from the east, which they saw as directed at the new revolutionary government there. They printed and distributed leaflets, in English and Yiddish, that condemned the President and the government for this action, called upon the workers of the world to awake and put down capitalism, and urged American workers to engage in a general strike, with particular language directed to those working in munitions factories.[9] The new statute forbade criticism of the government, provocation of resistance to the United States, and interference with the production of war materials.

In what is for our purposes its most interesting provision, the statute

8. 250 U.S. 616 (1919).

9. For a full statement of the facts and background, see Richard Polenberg, *Fighting Faiths*, 43–81 (1987).

also made it criminal willfully to "urge, incite, or advocate any curtailment of production [of war materials] ... with intent by such curtailment to cripple or hinder the United States in the prosecution of the war."[10]

The language of "intention" enabled the defendants to make an argument not available in *Schenck,* namely that their efforts were intended not to interfere with the war against Germany, as charged, but to stop the independent American invasion of Russia.

The defendants' claim was apparently an honest one: their real concern was for the new socialist government in Russia, not for the German regime, for which they bore no affection whatever. But the Court rejected it: "It will not do to say, as is now argued, that the only intent of these defendants was to prevent injury to the Russian cause. Men must be held to have intended, and to be accountable for, the effects which their acts were likely to produce."[11] And even if their primary purpose was to help Russia, the Court went on, they called for a general strike, especially in the munitions industry, which would obviously hinder the war effort against Germany.[12]

Here I want to call upon our earlier reading of the Model Penal Code to ask how one trained under it might respond to the Court's reasoning. Remember that under the Code's analysis the question would be: What degree of culpability should the statute be read to require with respect to each of its material elements?

The Court's first formulation, that men should be held accountable for the effects their acts were likely to produce, really amounts to a holding that negligence is the proper degree of culpability with respect to "curtailment." But in its opinion the Court simply erases the distinction between crimes requiring true purpose, as conspiracy and attempt normally do, and those based on negligence or recklessness, as in certain forms of manslaughter. This is consistent with the criminal law of the day, but disturbing to the reader who comes to it from the Model Penal Code, especially in light of the explicit intent requirement in the statute,

10. Act of May 16, 1918, ch. 75, 40 Stat. 553. Unlike the "obstruction" statute, this statute overtly punishes a speech act and could therefore be thought to present its own first amendment problems. But neither the Court nor Holmes saw it this way.

11. *Abrams,* 250 U.S. at 621.

12. *Id.* at 623.

which reads: "with intent by such curtailment to cripple or hinder the United States in the prosecution of the war."[13]

The Court's second formulation seems, without acknowledging it, to be saying something quite different, and more justifiable: that in this case the defendants could be found to have a true intention to hinder, since it was their hope and object to achieve a state of affairs—the interference with the production of munitions—that they knew would hinder the government. This would be a holding, assuming the distinctions of the Model Penal Code applied, that the "intent" requirement could be met by knowledge as well as purpose. In the Court's view that they were doing this for a motive not contemplated by the statute, the protection of Russia, is irrelevant—just as it is irrelevant if the reason an escaping criminal deliberately shoots and happens to kill a policeman is not hostility or a positive desire to kill, but simply a wish to escape, for which the killing seems to be necessary. But for this theory to work one would think that the jury must have been given an appropriate instruction about intention as including knowledge, authorizing them to convict specifically on that ground.

What these two formulations together reveal—and they have the support of much else in the criminal law of the time—is to the eyes of one educated by the Code a fundamental weakness of understanding and analysis. This is crude and undifferentiating thought, the Code lawyer would say; it not only reaches questionable results, it fails even to identify or address with clarity the fundamental issue of the proper degree of culpability, blurring the distinctions between negligence, recklessness, knowledge, and true purpose.

---

13. Act of May 16, 1918, ch. 75, 40 Stat. at 553. The Court's position on "intention," odd though it is to one trained in the Model Penal Code, is not eccentric but seems to reflect the criminal law thinking of the time. Here is Wharton, for example: "When there is a general intent to do evil . . . of which evil the wrong actually done may be looked upon as a probable incident, then the party having such general intent is to be regarded as having intended the particular wrong." See Francis Wharton (with James M. Kerr), *A Treatise on Criminal Law*, Vol. I, 202 (11th ed. 1912). And even today the felony murder rule rests on something like this analytic basis.

Holmes's Opinion in Dissent

Holmes, in dissent, analyzes the case with much greater care. The first two counts, based on new statutory provisions which today we would plainly hold unconstitutional, charge conspiracies to publish abusive language about the form of government of the United States and to publish language intended to bring that form of government into contempt. Holmes does not suggest that these provisions are unconstitutional, but he says that there is nothing in the record to support conviction under either count.[14] With respect to the count charging advocacy of curtailment of the war effort, he says that the record will simply not support the finding of an intention to cripple or hinder the United States in the prosecution of the war.

But as a general matter he concurs in the way of thinking the Court's opinion reflects, saying:

> I am aware of course that the word intent as vaguely used in ordinary legal discussion means no more than knowledge at the time of the act that the consequences said to be intended will ensue. Even less than that will satisfy the general principle of civil and criminal liability. A man may have to pay damages, may be sent to prison, at common law might be hanged, if at the time of his act he knew facts from which common experience showed that the consequences would follow, whether he individually could foresee them or not.[15]

Like the Court, Holmes here elides the distinction, later to be drawn so clearly by the Model Penal Code, between intent and negligence (as he also did programmatically in *The Common Law*[16]).

What makes this case different for him is that it is not a common law case but a statutory one. And "this statute must be taken to use its words in a strict and accurate sense,"[17] not only because it is a statute, but because otherwise it would be absurd. For if read otherwise it would

14. *Abrams*, 250 U.S. at 624 (Holmes, J., dissenting).

15. *Id.* at 626–27.

16. See *The Common Law*, 49–51, 108–09 (1881) (reprint by Dover Publications, 1991).

17. *Abrams*, 250 U.S. at 627 (Holmes, J., dissenting).

punish a patriot who argued successfully against what he thought were wasteful war expenditures, say on airplanes, which later came to be seen as essential to the prosecution of the war.[18] The statute should therefore require what we, educated by the Model Penal Code, would call a true purpose to cripple or hinder the war effort, and that cannot be established by this record.

Notice how the way of reading established by the Model Penal Code would have clarified the issues. It would have repudiated as an analytic mishmash the view of the Court that "men must be held to have intended, and to be accountable for, the effects which their acts were likely to produce,"[19] saying that of course people can be punished for negligently or recklessly producing a socially harmful result, but that they should be so punished only under a statute, or other rule, that articulates those degrees of culpability, certainly not under a statute that requires "intent." What is more, they should be punished much less severely than one who intends the harm, or knows that it will flow from his conduct. Once true "intent" is required, the question, as Holmes says, is whether the record will support such a finding, which may in turn depend upon the difference, perhaps assumed but not articulated by the Court, between intent and motive.[20]

What happens here, then, is this. Without fully seeing the challenge to his own established views about the objective basis for criminal as well as civil liability, Holmes seizes upon the language of intention in the statute to move him, and us, in the direction ultimately taken by the Code.

In doing so he exemplifies the kind of legal knowledge that consists

---

18. *Id.*

19. *Abrams,* 250 U.S. at 621.

20. Holmes's response to the argument that the defendants' ultimate "motive" is irrelevant if they actually intended to curtail production is to say:

> It may be obvious, and obvious to the actor, that the consequence will follow, and he may be liable for it even if he regrets it, but he does not do the act with intent to produce it unless the aim to produce it is the proximate motive of the specific act, although there may be some deeper motive behind it.

Id. at 627 (Holmes, J., dissenting). This language leaves open the argument that the defendants' "proximate motive" was in fact to curtail production and that this would constitute "intent" as Holmes defines it. Even so, Holmes may be justified in his position here, on the grounds that the jury was not properly charged and it would therefore be irrelevant if there were evidence from which they could find for the government on what Holmes calls "proximate motive."

of an art of language and imagination, here including the capacity to transform his own inherited materials of thought in a disciplined and persuasive way. More than that: by what seems like an accident, his insistence on one criminal law rule over another—requiring real proximity, and a true intention to bring about the harm in question—has the effect of protecting a certain kind of speech, speech that expresses general ideas or values, or advocates or criticizes policies.

Out of this shift in criminal law doctrine emerges the beginning of first amendment thought on the Court. Holmes here makes something out of almost nothing, and what he makes is of enormous interest and importance.

It is important that Holmes's intention requirement is based upon the language of the statute, not the Constitution. As a constitutional matter he explicitly reaffirms the "clear and present danger" language of *Schenck*:

> I do not doubt for a moment that by the same reasoning that would justify punishing persuasion to murder, the United States constitutionally may punish speech that *produces or is intended to produce* a clear and imminent danger that it will bring about forthwith certain substantive evils that the United States constitutionally may seek to prevent.[21]

Holmes here makes plain that Congress could, if it wanted to, punish speech that actually "produces" harm by a standard less protective than intention or purpose—for example under a statute that prohibited the reckless curtailment of war production. But Congress must make such a choice explicitly, and here it has made the opposite choice, to require "intent."

This judgment greatly narrows the scope of Holmes's implied constitutional rule, which would thus require intention only in uncompleted crimes, such as attempt or conspiracy, not in completed crimes, which the legislature is free to punish under a lower standard. If you look at this case with the eyes of the criminal lawyer, then, Holmes is arguing that the first amendment requires a small shift in a rule (requiring purpose not negligence or recklessness) governing a small piece of the universe of

21. *Id.* (emphasis added).

criminal statutes (attempt and conspiracy), and then only when speech, or speech of a certain kind, is involved.

From the point of view of the first amendment lawyer, however, this minor shift in the degree of culpability in this small class of cases constitutes practically the entire universe of first amendment law at the time.

What happens next, though I think it could not easily have been predicted, is that the insistence by Holmes and Brandeis upon the "clear and present danger" test in a range of political cases ultimately makes the central issues of attempt and conspiracy law—proximity and intention—the central issues of first amendment analysis as well.

It need not have happened this way. Holmes might have started off his dissent in *Abrams,* for example, by assessing the social value of the kind of speech the defendants engaged in. If one were to think of freedom of speech as an individual right, it would be natural to begin with the speech itself, first judging its quality and character and then declaring that it is, or is not, protected.

But Holmes begins the other way round, not with the speech but with the harm, saying that the defendants did not come close enough to inflicting a harm against which the state has a right to protect itself. As a matter of criminal law this reasoning could apply to other conduct that was also too remote from harm, regardless of its social value, such as purchasing a weapon with which one intended to commit a crime or ordering plans for a building one intended to bomb.

Would Holmes draw distinctions among different kinds of conduct and speech that are all equally remote from harm and, if so, how and why? Does it matter if the conduct consists only of words, or words of a certain sort? These are questions that this part of Holmes's opinion implicitly raises but does not answer.

The Beginnings of First Amendment Law

At this point, Holmes shifts voice and direction, looking now at the case as a whole:

> In this case sentences of twenty years imprisonment have been imposed for the publishing of two leaflets that I believe the defendants had as much right to publish as the Government has to publish the Constitution of the United States now vainly invoked by them.[22]

---

22. *Id.* at 629.

No longer making a technical analysis of the statutory language or of the charges of the respective counts, Holmes now displays a grasp of the whole; and he conceives of the defendants not simply as having a case against them fail for want of proof, but as having a "right," a right to publish.

The first amendment here makes its first real appearance, protecting in his words "the creed that they avow—a creed that I believe to be the creed of ignorance and immaturity . . . but which . . . no one has a right even to consider in dealing with the charges before the Court."[23] Again we have the word "right," here negatived by the Court, affirmed by Holmes on behalf of the defendants, a right that is now the right to a "creed"—a creed that everyone knows, as Holmes *almost* says, was the true object of condemnation in this case, and others like it. We are taking our first steps into a different world.

Then comes his famous paragraph on the purposes of the first amendment, beginning with what may seem an odd concession: that if you are confident in your premises and your power, you will naturally "express your wishes in law and sweep away all opposition."[24] In this sense, "persecution for the expression of opinions" is "perfectly logical."[25] Holmes articulates here an image of government as a kind of tyranny, based upon the premise that the winner takes all. Victory, if total, brings total power. This instinct is his starting point. But he expresses this vision only to repudiate it on the basis of experience, to distinguish it from our way of imagining both our government and our society:

> But when men have realized that time has upset many fighting faiths, they may come to believe even more than they believe the very foundations of their own conduct that the ultimate good desired is better reached by free trade in ideas—that the best test of truth is the power of the thought to get itself accepted in the competition of the market, and that truth is the only ground upon which their wishes safely can be carried out. That at any rate is the theory of our Constitution. It is an experiment, as all life is an experiment. Every year if not every day we have to wager our salvation upon some prophecy based upon imperfect knowledge. While that experiment is part

23. *Id.* at 629–30.
24. *Id.* at 630.
25. *Id.*

> of our system I think that we should be eternally vigilant against attempts to check the expression of opinions that we loathe and believe to be fraught with death, unless they so imminently threaten immediate interference with the lawful and pressing purposes of the law that an immediate check is required to save the country.[26]

While much can be said in favor of, and against, the view Holmes here expresses of the first amendment, his main achievement is to express any view at all. No other Justice had done so.[27] Whatever the first amendment was then thought to be, the Court had established no way of thinking that would make it relevant to a criminal conspiracy plainly within the zone of congressional power, as this one seemed to be.

In the terms I suggested earlier, Holmes finds a way to give meaning to the text by imagining the world in which it occurs, including himself and others within it, in a new and coherent way; it is this act of imagination that is the center of this famous paragraph. He no longer sees this case as like one in which the state punishes persuasion to murder. What is at stake here, rather, is what he calls a "creed," consisting of "ideas" and

---

26. *Id.*

27. As is well known, Judge Learned Hand, in *Masses Publishing Co. v. Patten*, 244 F. 535 (S.D.N.Y. 1917), had struggled with the question, and took the view that speech that fell short of "counsel[ing] or advis[ing] others to violate the law" should be protected. *Id.* at 540. In this opinion he defines the key terms thus: "To counsel or advise a man to an act is to urge upon him either that it is his interest or his duty to do it." *Id.*

Instead of asking the jury a question of "proximity," as Holmes did in *Schenck*, Hand sees the central issue as the character or quality of the speech, or what we might call the nature of the speech act. During the interval between *Schenck* and *Abrams*, he urged these views on Holmes in correspondence, but Holmes saw very little difference between the two formulations. Sheldon M. Novick, *Honorable Justice: The Life of Oliver Wendell Holmes*, 473 n.87 (1989); see also Polenberg, *Fighting Faiths*, 218–19. In "Freedom of Speech in War Time," 32 *Harvard Law Review* 932 (1919) Zechariah Chafee, Jr., argued that Holmes's clear and present danger test could be construed as meaning something very close to Hand's formulation and that this would provide the beginning of a rational principle upon which first amendment jurisprudence could be founded.

The standard view is that Holmes was influenced by Chafee, with whom he conversed, as well as by Hand, and that this explains the sea change between the two cases. Novick is doubtful, not sure that there is such a sea change: Holmes reaffirms *Schenck* in explicit terms in *Abrams*, and rests his opinion in *Abrams* on a ground not available in *Schenck*, namely the statutory provision requiring an intention to curtail production. See Novick at 473 n.87. My own interest here is less in explaining why the shift in Holmes's position occurred than in trying to understand what he made his language mean.

"thoughts." He thus separates out from the world of standard criminal law cases what he sees to be the material of a first amendment case.

For without quite realizing it, he found in *Schenck* a point of criminal law analysis with which to begin thinking about the first amendment. His clear and present danger test is in its origins simply a statement of an intention and proximity requirement for attempt and conspiracy liability. But he and others will now and later give it enormous resonance in speech cases. Having made the beginning he did in *Schenck*, he moves in this paragraph to a statement that will begin to explain and justify his instincts.

Difficulty and Paradox

What he says here can be criticized, of course. The exchange of ideas, or their competition, is not really a market, in which people are paying more or less for what they value;[28] what he has in mind is closer to what may be his deepest image of human life, the process of evolution by the survival of the fittest. But survival is a test of power, not of truth, and we all know that false, despicable, and dangerous ideologies or ideas can thrive for a long time.

Particularly in the field of ethics and justice, there is no reason to think that we always move progressively towards a better world. Holmes's view that significant speech consists of "ideas" or "thoughts" is highly limiting, for it tends to find the value of speech in its reified products, when one might think that its value is in fact processual, subtle, and far too protean to be reduced to something called "ideas."

It is in fact one of the great merits of this very paragraph that it cannot be boiled down to a single idea, or concept, which can be simply carried

---

28. And to say that speech is like a market is not to say that it should be unregulated, for our tradition is that the government has broad powers to regulate actual markets of a commercial kind, powers broader by far than it has to interfere with what we think of as individual rights specifically guaranteed by the Constitution. And there are real questions about the freedom and efficiency of our own "market in ideas," if one uses such language, for it can be seen to be dominated by some voices and to exclude others. But Holmes was not really arguing for the systematic extension of market thought into this field; rather he was trying to find a way to express, through a metaphor, the importance of freedom of speech to society as a whole, building perhaps on Chafee's insistence—well chosen, if his idea was indeed to influence Holmes—that there is a "social interest" in freedom of speech, as well as an "individual" one, a social interest that Chafee, like Holmes here, characterizes in terms of "truth." *See* Chafee, *supra* chapter one, note 1, at 956–59.

away by the reader; it is itself too complex, too tension-filled, too alive, to permit such treatment.

But these are small points: the great thing is that Holmes found a way to imagine the world in such a way as to give the first amendment meaning and scope, which no other Justice had yet done—and a way of imagining that is not ideological or mechanical in character.

For his imagined universe is populated with people who are striving to understand and speak, disagreeing to the point of war, claiming power, asserting truth, and he says that this activity, in which he is himself engaged, in this very paragraph and throughout his work as a Justice, is one that must be in its nature local and provisional. Just when we are most sure we are right, we must recognize that we may be wrong; and not only about matters of truth, as he puts it, but about matters of justice as well.

There is a paradox deep in Holmes's opinion. As I suggested above, one could approach this case by thinking about the value of the speech in question—its importance to the speaker and to the world—but Holmes treats the issue primarily as one of proximity to a cognizable harm. Although he sets forth a statement of the aims of the first amendment and of the value of speech, in operation his opinion works like an old-fashioned due process analysis, which focuses more upon injury to a claimed state interest than on a delineation of "rights." This approach is consistent with the skeptical strain in this opinion and in Holmes's thought more generally, for it expresses a sense that one cannot know, cannot judge, the ultimate value of any particular act of speech.

We are always situated in our interests, in our culture, and the whole point of the first amendment, to one part of Holmes's mind, is to establish a process that will lead to changes we cannot foresee and would not, in the present cast of our minds, approve, and thus to changes in our own ways of thinking and perceiving.

The paradox is that this skepticism produces a principle that is far more tolerant of speech in general, and tolerant of far more kinds of speech, than would an explicit analysis of what one might think of as specifically first amendment interests and concerns—focusing for example on the value of a particular expression or type of expression—for Holmes's principle does not easily draw lines of relative value among speech acts.

One doubts whether Holmes means this skepticism as strongly as he seems to say, for at other points in the opinion he is, to say the least, unafraid to make and articulate judgments of value. Indeed, his tolerance of the speech in this case depends partly upon his sense that it is really of no consequence—if the defendants were not "puny anonymities,"[29] as he calls them, but represented a serious threat, his skeptical tolerance might well disappear, as he implicitly acknowledges. But the thread of thought he establishes here is still with us.[30] And the habit of mind Holmes manifests—of thinking in terms of the proximity of harm to already recognized interests—is also at work today, for good or ill, in what we call "hate speech" and "pornography" cases, where we find it very hard to admit that the social evil the government has a right to prevent lies in the speech itself, as opposed to the "interests" that we claim, or deny, that the speech threatens or injures. If we had begun differently we might think differently now.[31]

An Act of Imagination

I referred at the beginning to the view of the rabbi that knowledge of Jewish law could not be reduced to the knowledge of rules, or even to understanding what conduct the rules required, but consisted as well in knowledge of who you are, in relation both to the larger community and to the God of Israel whose gift these laws are.

In constitutional discourse there is no God, of course, but there is something as it were analogous, for we endow the Framers with a largeness of vision and depth of wisdom that enable us to think of the Constitution in the idealized way we do, and ought to do.

---

29. *Abrams,* 250 U.S. at 629 (Holmes, J., dissenting).

30. And is still subject to doubt: would *Brandenburg v. Ohio,* 395 U.S. 444 (1969), the case that established the most protective form of the "clear and present danger" test, really apply to speech that had no political or social substance at all but was rather part of a garden-variety conspiracy to commit murder or extortion? Even if it were cast in the form of "ideas": "the only good cop is a dead cop," or "nothing is more important than the honor of the family"?

31. Or think of *Abrams* itself, in which Holmes's judgment seems to rest in large part on the "absurdity" of a reading of the statute that would punish the patriot who argued, wrongly it turns out, against the production of a certain kind of armament. *Abrams,* 250 U.S. at 627 (Holmes, J., dissenting). But this imagined result is not the only possibility: one less skeptical than Holmes might be willing to draw a line between the kind of speech imagined there and the kind of speech engaged in by the defendants in *Abrams,* both in terms of form—one calling for a strike, the other arguing the merits of a position—and in terms of intention or motive, one disregarding (at best) the nation's interest in the war, the other seeking to advance it.

We cannot read the Constitution except as a text that has an author, and hence as having a kind of meaning that cannot be reduced to rule, or policy, or system—a meaning that depends upon a sense of character and identity, in the community and in oneself; upon what I have called a way of imagining the world, and oneself and others within it, that will make possible coherent speech and significant action. This is what Holmes achieves: a sense of the nation as having a character, a character like the one he gives himself in his prose—confident of its views, ready to act upon them, but at that very moment aware that it may be mistaken, that a voice it is inclined to sweep away may be telling the truth.

Holmes is here teaching us that, at its deepest, legal knowledge is imaginative in character. Not just imaginative, performative, for Holmes's own opinion, in dissent, is an enactment of the theory he articulates: it is an effort by him to put into competition with others an "idea" necessarily provisional, in the hope that its truth will ultimately be accepted by others—as indeed happens, for this paragraph becomes perhaps our most important single statement of the nature and purposes of the first amendment.

As I suggest above, this passage cannot actually be reduced to a single proposition or image; far too complex for that, it is what I would call "writing" rather than an "idea," a way of presenting essential tensions in a momentary order. Yet it is offered in competition with other writings, as an example to be read and understood and learned from, one that may affect our own thinking and writing too. And if we are persuaded by this performance, we affirm not only his position but the very process he describes and in which he, and we, participate.

Holmes's performance is not strategic or instrumental, but authentic, expressing not only "ideas" that can in a sense be shared and passed around and argued about, but the deepest nerve of his own mind and imagination, in a voice that is distinctively his own. His articulation of the deep tensions that mark his mind—between skepticism and faith, brute power and idealization, tolerance and judgment, dominance and truth—is not in fact a weakness of his opinion, any more than the tensions at work in the Model Penal Code are weaknesses, but a gift to us, and part of the gift is that the tensions cannot be resolved. He means what he says, and we know it; and his writing has the force it does in large measure by virtue of that fact.

At the end he tells us: "I regret that I cannot put into more impressive words my belief that in their conviction upon this indictment the defendants were deprived of their rights under the Constitution of the United States."[32] He talks not only about the beliefs of others, and their fighting faiths, he has beliefs of his own. He shows us how it is possible to mean what you say in the language of the law. He speaks from the center. A person writing about the first amendment needs to have a way of imagining what it means that human beings have language, and can think and speak; what it means, or can mean, to be a speaking person, including in the law. This is what Holmes seeks in different ways to define, and what he asks us in our turn to define as well. He makes an effort to show us the kind of speech to which we can aspire, the speech made possible by our freedom.

This opinion written in favor of freedom of speech does not take the position that all speech is equally valuable or good; it is not nonjudgmental; quite the contrary, it sets forth a ground in its own performance for the criticism of speech, including not only the speech at issue in the particular case, but the speech of other Justices, of lawyers, of all of us in fact who engage in the legal and political processes of reasoned debate.

The "legal knowledge" he represents to us is thus a capacity of mind and language; he seeks to teach it to us; in the nature of things this cannot be done in a mechanical or ideological or propositional way, as a teaching of material; instead, he offers a demonstration of human possibility for meaningful speech—for speech that is meant—in the law.

Legal Knowledge as a Writer's Knowledge

I mean by these readings of the Model Penal Code and Supreme Court opinions to suggest something of a general kind about the nature of legal knowledge, namely that at its heart it is a kind of writer's knowledge: the knowledge of legal language and the art of using it, criticizing it, transforming it, all with the aim of working out a way of imagining the world, and oneself and others within it, that will enable us to speak coherently about what we call justice.

As we just saw in our reading of Holmes's opinion, the writing required is not simply a matter of technique, but a matter of character and identity. Justice requires us to find open and respectful ways of imag-

32. *Id.* at 631.

ining ourselves and each other. Our law is of course not religious law, but like religious law it calls for more than a learning of rules, or rote obedience, or technical skill—it calls for thought and speech of a whole-minded kind. An important part of what the rabbi said about Jewish law is true of our secular law as well: we must know who we are in reading it and in writing it, and what it calls upon us to do and to be. We need to know what is distinctive about our history, for good and ill: the nature of the experiment of government of the people, by the people, and for the people, and of the forces that threaten it.

This kind of writing or speaking comes from the center. Its coherence is not a matter of the consistency of an intellectual system, but the consistency of an identity, a mind, a voice. In both legislature and judge it requires the capacity to live with what one does not yet understand and cannot manage. Both Holmes and the Model Penal Code at their best speak from a place defined by real and serious thought, which nonetheless recognizes what cannot be understood or stated.

It is not only the Constitution that requires this response in us: any statute does the same, as we saw with the Model Penal Code, as does any case. All law calls upon us to act, not merely to repeat or invoke, but to make something new. Of course we work with old materials—as this very chapter retells old and familiar stories—but it is our task as lawyers to make something with a quality of freshness and immediacy, directed to the present moment.

The art of writing cannot be reduced to a program that can be taught and applied, certainly not to a set of tricks or techniques. It must be learned as other arts are learned: by practice, by critical examination—by more practice and more reflection; by reading the works of others and discussing them, then returning to our own work; by attending to the nature of the languages we are given to use, their strengths and limits, capacities and constraints; and by thinking of the ways in which we define ourselves and others, as minds, as institutional and social actors, as members of a community and culture.

My aim in these two chapters has accordingly not been to work out a method either for the performance or for the teaching of the art I point to, but simply to render more particular, and perhaps more insistent, an intuition that I think most lawyers also have, that the life of the law is full of opportunities and occasions, never perfectly realized, for imagination, for invention, for creation in language, or for what I call "writing."

I will only add that I think this fact should be closer to the center of our attention as teachers and scholars, in law schools and law firms alike, than perhaps it has been. What the writers examined here achieve is not merely a literary excellence, but a legal excellence, and we all need to think about what that is, or can be.

Several times in this chapter I have spoken of the imagination, and for me that is the root and nerve of my subject. I think that the deepest specifically human need is the need to claim meaning for experience,[33] and that our ability to do this is dependent upon our capacity to imagine the world, and ourselves and others within it, in a sufficiently coherent way to make such claims possible.

This is not something that can be done easily, or done once and for always. We necessarily meet impediments, in our nature, in our culture, in our language, in the limits and corruptions of our own minds. The art of making meaning is an art of coming to terms with these conditions of our lives, in the law and out of it. Holmes and the Model Penal Code show us how to do something, but it is up to us to do it afresh, for ourselves and our contemporaries, in our own language and in our own situation. Like them, we—as teachers and writers both—should be prepared to make new versions of our inheritance, good for our time and for our minds, recognizing that what we say too will need to be revised in turn, as we join those who have come before and will come after, each of us using as writers the materials of law to try to make sense of our experience in a continuing and collective effort to imagine justice into reality.

We have read only bits and pieces of Holmes's opinions, but it may not be too early to ask how you would characterize his achievement in them. Is it that he comes to the right understanding of the first amendment, perhaps as expressed especially in his phrase "clear and present danger"? Or that he somehow turns criminal law into constitutional law? Or that, more generally, he turns what is old into something new and alive? All three at once?

Can you explain how he gives the law new life here?

So far as you can tell from these passages, do you agree with me that his

33. See *The Edge of Meaning*, especially at xi–xiv (2001).

achievement here is largely one of character and identity? Could you explain how that is so? Another way to put that question might be to ask: Does he mean what he says? How would you begin to answer such a question?

Here is another line of thought. In a sense the structural heart of law is respect for the authority of decisions made by others. Thus a judge must respect decisions made by the legislature or by private parties (say in a contract) or by other courts acting within their respective zones of authority; similarly, all legal actors must respect decisions made by the Framers of the Constitution. But the act of respecting is harder than it sounds, the authorities in question have first to be identified, sometimes a contested matter, then interpreted, also often contested, with reasons given on both sides. The court or other legal actor must construe, and in a sense constitute, the statements claimed to be authoritative. In facing these questions the court turns to history, to policy, to the almost always complex set of statements claimed to be authoritative, in an effort to make sense of the whole. So far as you can tell, how does Holmes engage in this process?

Is his view of law merely technical, or does he see its ultimate concern as justice? If the latter, how does he imagine and make real his sense of justice?

Does it matter whether the literary and cultural form we call the judicial opinion is done well or badly? Why? To whom?

3

What's Wrong with Our Talk about Race?

In the two opening chapters I tried to show how the Model Penal Code and Justice Holmes in their different ways demonstrate excellence in legal thought and judgment. In the present chapter I act as a critic of the law, arguing that it should think and talk differently from the way it does about race. I am trying here to correct the law, as it were, to make it better. In this effort I must myself of necessity try to demonstrate what I have called excellence, an effort that will by its nature invite you to do the same in your response—whether approving or disapproving—to what I have written.

That is, I must myself necessarily try to exemplify, in my own writing, the kind of law that I admire, the law that I think is the subject of threats from many directions. Not that what I do or say is beyond argument; far from it; but this argument, carried on in the right way, might itself be a way of keeping law alive. As you read, keep your critical faculties alert and engaged, for in doing so you will be participating in an essential activity of legal thinking and expression. You will be helping to keep law alive.

While you find yourself in conversation with the chapter, agreeing in one place, disagreeing in another, wanting more information somewhere else, not sure of the relevance of some information it does provide, ask how you would characterize the activity in which you yourself are engaged, your version, that is, of the activity of law. What does it mean to our country and culture that conversations like this may take place, and that they be done well?

The major issue I address here is the relation that can and should exist between our legal language and our language of race. What is the law to do with the impossible way of talking and thinking about people that our language of race offers? We are committed to equality as a value, but what can it mean here? There is no easy answer, to put it mildly, but in this chapter I will state my own views on a part of the problem.

To think about how the law should talk about race requires a broader reach of mind than I have so far suggested, since we have to think about race itself, which is a social and historical and political fact of immense significance in our national life, both morally and practically. Race is right at the center of our experience in this country, and our question is: How should law talk about it?

ONE OF THE MAJOR ACHIEVEMENTS of the *Michigan Law Review* during its first century was a Symposium entitled, "Legal Storytelling" published in 1989.[1] In this chapter I build upon the idea of Symposium, connecting law and narrative and the imagination, but I do so in a rather different way from any of those who wrote for it.

Huckleberry Finn

People sometimes talk as though narrative is invariably a liberating or "subversive" mode of thought, when of course it is not: stories can be as authoritarian, reactionary, closed-minded, and self-satisfied as any other form of discourse.[2] But I think it is also true that the narrative imagination has its own ways of working that are inconsistent with more theoretical or abstract forms of speech.[3]

Sometimes in telling a story we may find that it takes on a life of its

1. "Legal Storytelling," 87 *Michigan Law Review* 2073 (1989). An earlier version of this chapter was published as "What's Wrong with our Talk About Race? On History, Particularity, and Affirmative Action," 100 *Michigan Law Review* 1927 (2002). In preparing this chapter I have for the most part not updated footnotes, and I have deleted some of them.

2. See L. H. LaRue, "Stories versus Theories," 14 *Cardozo L. Rev.* 121, 134–36 (1992).

3. See *The Legal Imagination*, 858–926 (1973, 2018).

own, leading us to places we had not imagined and presenting problems of which we had been not consciously aware. This often happens, to take an extremely minor example, in the drafting of law school examinations, and I think it happens in larger and more important ways as well.

Think for example of *Huckleberry Finn*. My sense is that in shifting from the traditional third person narrator, as used in *Tom Sawyer*, to writing in the voice of this utterly marginal boy called Huckleberry, Twain was mainly thinking of the comic and satiric possibilities of the shift. Huck is a social idiot, who perceives everything in a kind of mixed literal and superstitious way: his ignorance of what we all know makes him look foolish, but his fresh perceptions of the silliness of our world often make us look foolish too. As I imagine it, under Twain's original plan the reader and author alike could feel comfortably superior to both Huck and Petersburg (Twain's name for Hannibal, Missouri).

But as the story proceeds it gets out of control: Huck becomes a center of moral life, his friendship with Jim is real—by far the best thing in his life—and Jim himself emerges as a person of extraordinary moral and emotional quality, able to help Huck grow and change. I will not now rehearse the familiar story, but want only to point out that after the famous moment in chapter sixteen at which Huck refuses to turn Jim in to the slave-hunters, the novel comes to a halt.

Huck has come to recognize that Jim is his friend, in a real sense the only friend he has ever had, and Twain has no way to imagine the next step in their story. In fact he stopped writing the book at this point, and when he came back to it three years later he was able to proceed only by separating Huck and Jim, and by presenting Huck as though he did not know what he learned in chapter sixteen.

It turns out that there is no way Twain can imagine the relation between this boy and this man in the social world in which they are placed, the only social world available. I think we could not imagine a life for them in that world either, and that this is a fact full of the deepest social significance.[4]

In one sense, I suppose, this was a real surprise to Twain, a frustration of his comic and satiric intentions. In another sense it was of course no

---

4. For a fuller statement of what I suggest about *Huckleberry Finn*, see *The Edge of Meaning*, chapter two (2001).

surprise at all, for the story came from within Twain as an expression of a deep and troubling truth at the center of his own experience.

The Problem of Race-Talk

I mean all of this as prelude to an effort of my own to raise a question with which my own imagination, and I think that of the law, cannot adequately deal, namely the meaning of what we call "race" in our world, especially in the context of "affirmative action." Race is of course the topic on which *Huckleberry Finn* ran aground, and I think we do too—or at least I do.

I believe a large part of the problem is the way we tell the story of race in our culture, so in a small way I shall carry forward the theme of the Symposium to which I referred at the outset, where several of the writers spoke specifically to narratives about race in America.[5] At the same time I shall be engaging in more analytic modes of thought as well, though these turn out to have the property that stories often have, namely that they bring me in the end to a point I had not imagined at the beginning.

My starting point is a sense I have that there is something awry in the way we in the law talk both about race in general and about affirmative action in particular, something simply missing, or misrepresented. The legal arguments and judicial opinions I read have in general a smooth and plausible and honorable feel, but I have a nagging sense of something deeply wrong, as deeply wrong perhaps as what Twain discovered in his own way of imagining the world. I cannot prove that I am right, or even say with any clarity why I feel what I do, or what it is that is missing or wrong. This chapter is thus really a tentative exploration of an intuition.

It contains some factual assertions, some analytic points, some normative judgments, but it is meant to be something different from the sum of these elements and not reducible to them. You might say it is about the way I—and we—imagine certain things: our history, especially our racial history; the role of race today, especially the racial line between those we call white and black; and the practice of affirmative action, especially in the university.

5. See the papers by Patricia Williams, David Luban, Milner Ball, Mari Matsuda, Derrick Bell, Richard Delgado, and Clark Cunningham.

This kind of work has an ineradicably personal element, for our imaginings are always individual as well as shared. I am trying to say how things really look to me, and how they look is a function of my own experience and capacity and perception.[6] It is necessarily the case that they will look somewhat different to others, and this is all to the good.

As a matter of form, the first half of the chapter will develop the intuition I spoke of above, asking the reader whether or not he or she shares my perceptions; the second half will identify certain consequences that might flow from this intuition.

My fundamental point in casting the chapter as I do is that even to ask the question, how we think of race in the law, is to draw attention to an act specifically of the imagination; and that thinking about race necessarily has some of the features of narrative, including the presentation of real or imagined characters against a background, engaged in a sequence of actions and events for which a meaning is claimed—and often a meaning that works as something of a surprise.

I am speaking here of the problem of white talk about race, since for these purposes legal talk is mostly white talk.[7] For decades, even centu-

---

6. What I am trying to say here is difficult to articulate. An analogy might help. If you look at a series of great portraits, say by Rembrandt, or facial studies that are not formally portraits, say by Vermeer, you naturally find yourself trying to understand the person whose image is before you. This is a matter of reading tiny signs in the face—evidence of tension in the cheek or quizzicality in a partly raised eyebrow or petulance in the curve of a lip. If the painter has done his job well you have a sense of the person as real, with depth and complexity and a character you can begin to grasp. For him to do this, the painter has to master, perhaps without ever being able to make his knowledge explicit, the ways we read faces of real people in the world. This is a capacity we all have; and it is one way by which we decide whether to trust or mistrust another, and by which we form our expectations about their intelligence or sense of humor. (Think of our experience of what we would call an intelligent face.) Yet I at least cannot render this knowledge explicit. This is real knowledge, but it lives at the line between the conscious and the subconscious, available as a ground for action but not as the stuff of intellectual analysis.

I think our perceptions of race, and what it means, work in much this way, intuitively, instantaneously, felt not as conclusions reached from evidence but as direct registers of the world. They are simultaneously created by our inarticulate beliefs—expectations, larger understandings—and themselves create such beliefs, all at a level that is only partly available to the conscious mind. This is in a sense where race happens and in the first part of this chapter I try to say something about what I perceive in myself and others in this dimension of life.

7. Of course there have been crucial contributions made by black lawyers and judges, but these have necessarily been contributions to a discourse largely shaped and maintained

ries, American blacks and Asians and Hispanics and Native Americans and others have tried to tell the story of race as they experience it, often with great eloquence and with considerable effect on particular readers, but with rather little effect on the law, or on the way most lawyers and judges think. In a modest way I am trying to say something brief, from my own perspective as a white person, about what I see when I look at the world of race and at the way we in the law talk about it.[8]

The National Narrative

It is important to see that narrative works at the public or political as well as at the local and particular level.[9] Indeed, as the rabbi would understand, a part of every lawyer's task is to tell the story of the law itself—including, when appropriate, the history of the nation and its culture—as well as the particular story of his or her client, and to do so in a way that both makes sense of the relevant material in each dimension and produces an essential coherence between the two stories themselves. This means that some of the problems and opportunities of narrative are present whenever the lawyer speaks, including about the law and its history.

Here is one highly reduced and familiar version of our national story about the racial line between white and black: once we had racial slavery; then we had the Civil War; then we had the great Civil War amendments, prohibiting slavery, protecting the right to vote against racial discrimination, and prohibiting all the states of the Union from denying any person "equal protection of the laws"; then we had Reconstruction, and its abandonment in 1877; then we had *Plessy* and Jim Crow; then we had *Brown*; then we had the Civil Rights Act of 1964, prohibiting discrimination on the grounds of race, not only against blacks but anyone, and finally the Voting Rights Act of 1965. It all makes up a story of gradual amelioration.[10] The large constitutional question still before us,

by whites.

8. Sometimes I will use the word "we" deliberately to mean "we white people," sometimes more inclusively. I hope the context will make clear which use I intend.

9. See, *e.g.*, David Luban, "Difference Made Legal: The Court and Dr. King," 87 *Michigan Law Review* 2152 (1989), comparing *Walker v. Birmingham*, 289 U.S 894 (1967) with Martin Luther King, "Letter from Birmingham Jail," in *Why We Can't Wait*, 77 (1963).

10. It is clear, however, that in our day we are experiencing a back-sliding into a world in which the expression of racial hatred and contempt by white people is significantly

especially in the affirmative action case, is what the language of "equal protection" is to mean.

The well-known judicial discourse that the Supreme Court has fashioned to give meaning to this language maintains that the central evil against which it is directed is what we call "racial discrimination," and that any state action that distributes benefits or burdens, or otherwise regulates, on the basis of race will be subject to what in the jargon of the day is called "strict scrutiny." This in turn means that a classification in state law based on race will be upheld only if it is "necessary" to the protection of a "compelling" state interest. Where the alleged vice is discrimination on the grounds of something other than race, but still presumptively improper—alienage, gender, sexual orientation—the classification is subject to a less severe but still substantial form of scrutiny. A similar analysis employs similar degrees of scrutiny when a state regulation interferes with a right thought to be more or less "fundamental," such as the right to vote or travel.

Where no such suspect classification or fundamental right is involved, the state can do pretty much as it will, subject only to the requirement that there be a "rational relation" between the regulation in question and a valid state interest. This is a system of thought and law that is meant to be rational, coherent, comprehensive, and neutral.

What of the case where a state uses racial classifications in an effort to *benefit* races that were previously disadvantaged by the law, for example in ensuring that a certain percentage of public contracts go to minority businesses, or in using racial identity as a factor in admitting students to public universities? The courts have for the most part analyzed these cases in the traditional way, by asking whether the action in question is "necessary" to advance a "compelling state interest." Both halves of the test are used in turn to attack such programs: it is argued that there is no compelling state interest served by them, and that, even if there is, the use of race-based classifications is not necessary to achieve it. On the other side, these propositions are denied, asserting for example a compelling state interest in the educational value of "diversity" and claiming that it can only be attained by affirmative action in admissions. The ensuing arguments are lengthy, passionate, and repetitive.

---

more common and widespread, more socially acceptable, than it has been for many years. Whether this movement will continue to intensify or subside, no one can predict.

This way of talking seems to me, as I said above, to be awry, to miss—or miscast—something crucial, and my question is what that is. Where have we gone wrong?

My own sense is that a large part of the problem lies in the extreme generality and abstractness of the language of analysis summarized above.

What Is Race?

At the most basic level, for example, I think there is something profoundly wrong with the use of the generic terms "race" and "minority" in the system of thought described above. For, as I perceive it at least, the situation of African Americans in our country is unique and makes unique claims upon us. I think the descendants of slaves have suffered a kind of abuse and discrimination that is qualitatively different from that experienced by any other minority or race, and continue to do so.[11]

Of course it is also true that, particularly in certain regions of the country, the definition of other groups by their "race"—including Mexican Americans, Puerto Ricans, Chinese Americans, Japanese Americans, and Native Americans—has become foundational for parts of our society, with much of the viciousness that racism entails, including material deprivation, legal disadvantage, social degradation, and psychological oppression.[12] And immigrants to this country frequently find themselves placed in racial boxes they did not know existed, with puzzling and dam-

---

11. For the expressions of the early view that the equal protection clause was really about the treatment of former slaves and nothing else, see *The Slaughterhouse Cases* and *Strauder v. West Virginia*, page 65 *infra*.

12. For an account of the relations among blacks, Mexicans, and poor whites in the Texas cotton belt, see Neil Foley, *The White Scourge* (1997). For an analysis of the role of "whiteness" in our culture, see David Roediger, *Towards the Abolition of Whiteness* (1994). Thomas Holt, *The Problem of Race in the 21st Century* (2000), is very good on tracing the deep continuities in racial attitudes and experiences that are at work beneath surface changes. For further data see Harvard Civil Rights Project, "Schools More Separate: Consequences of a Decade of Desegregation," quoted in *New York Times*, July 20, 2000, page A12, and Richard Morris and Michael H. Cottman, "Discrimination's Lingering Sting," *Washington Post*, June 22, 2001, page A1. Three other notes from newspapers read while I was first preparing this chapter:

(1) A study of 300,000 car loans by Vanderbilt professor Mark A. Cohen shows that blacks consistently pay more than whites, regardless of their credit histories. See "Car Study Suggests Dealer Bias," *St. Petersburg Times*, July 10, 2001, available at: http://vanderbilt.directtrak.com/fetch/index.cfm?n=35&s=99&o=33&c=143824&t=11&e=5264;

aging consequences.[13] In what I say here I do not mean in any way to disregard the experience of such groups or to minimize their claims. But I do think that the dehumanization of African Americans has been unique in its duration, its intensity, its legalization, and its ideology, and that honesty requires us to admit that this is so.

This is obviously no accident, for the present condition of African Americans is at least in part a consequence of their experience in our collective past, namely their forced subjection to a legalized form of slavery that was designed to destroy their cultures, their dignity, and their humanity. In this book, which is partly about the excellence that law can attain, it is important to add that this whole hideous regime was strictly regulated by law, our law.[14]

This is not only a factual story but a moral one, with unique moral consequences, for American human slavery was one of the greatest crimes ever committed by one people against another.[15]

This is not just my judgment, or ours, it was a national judgment,

---

(2) John Flesher, "Black Prison Population Out of Proportion," *Ann Arbor News*, August 1, 2001, page B4, reported that blacks make up 14% of the population of Michigan but 50% of the prison population;

(3) The Texas Defender Service reports that Texas has never executed a white person for the murder of a black person. See Bob Herbert, "Tainted Justice," *New York Times*, August 6, 2001, page A13.

13. See, *e.g.*, Ronald Takaki, *Strangers from a Different Shore: A History of Asian Americans* (rev. ed. 1998).

14. For more about what this fact meant for the law itself, see the discussion in chapter five, pages 128–130 *infra*.

15. Human slavery in our country—unlike Greek and Roman slavery, for example—was not merely a deprivation of liberty, or a system of forced labor, but a totalizing program of dehumanization aimed at destroying the sense that those subject to it were in any full sense human beings. They were denied the right to marry, to maintain families, to read, to meet or talk with people from the larger world, and so on, with the aim of reducing them to a condition that by a hideous tautology would justify the system of slavery itself: since we had made them little more than animals they could be treated as animals. For a collection of relevant materials, see *The Legal Imagination*, 439–512 (1973, 2018).

I am speaking here of the object and aim of slavery; the fact that those subject to it were able to maintain their humanity, wit, and wisdom was one of the great achievements of the human spirit. See Eugene Genovese, *Roll, Jordan, Roll: The World the Slaves Made* (1976). For a summary account of the world of slavery from which the American version derived, see David Brion Davis, "Slavery—White, Black, Christian, Muslim," *New York Review of Books*, July 5, 2001, pages 51–53, and David Brion Davis, "Looking at Slavery from Broader Perspectives," 105 *American Historical Review* 452 (2000). For an account of the practice of

reached in the most painful possible way. Slavery was, as Lincoln said, "somehow the cause" of our incredibly devastating Civil War—650,000 dead out of a population of thirty million[16]—and after victory the status of African Americans was the subject of the three great Civil War amendments. Thus the situation of African Americans is distinctive not only sociologically but historically, morally, and—of enormous consequence for legal talk about affirmative action—constitutionally. The use of "race" and "minority" as though these terms were universals with the same significance in every instance simply erases the special sociological, historical, moral, and constitutional status of African Americans.

The Unique Experience of African Americans

The same can be said, I think, about the word "discrimination" (or the phrase "invidious classification"), for as I suggest above I think the nature and character of the "discrimination" experienced by African Americans is different from any other in our national experience. In fact, although of course I cannot prove this, I believe that for most white Americans "race" really refers to the line between white and black. I am of course limited by my own experience, but I have never heard anyone express towards any other racial group the intense fear, fascination, loathing, and contempt that at various stages in my lifetime I have perceived to be frequently, though of course not universally, directed by whites at African Americans. While the explicit expressions of these feelings has become rarer over the past forty years, at least in the circles in which I move, there is something in my world that takes its place, namely meaningful silences, pauses, shifts in tones of voice, all expressive of a sense of

"convict leasing," which kept a least part of the population in something very like slavery until 1930, see Douglas A. Blackmon, "From Alabama's Past, Capitalism and Racism in a Cruel Partnership," *Wall Street Journal*, July 16, 2001, page A1.

I can myself remember white people who opposed integration talking of blacks in exactly the terms I suggest, as being less than fully human, with whom association on equal terms was unthinkable, intermarriage an abomination, like a form of bestiality. It was in part to resist this conception of who they were that so many escaped slaves thought it important to tell their story—to show, that is, that despite the ideology, and the attempts of the slave-owning South to create facts consistent with it, they were fully human, capable of thought and speech and feeling and imagination and moral sense, and able to write. See especially Frederick Douglass, *Autobiographies* (Library of America, Henry Louis Gates, Jr., ed., 1994).

16. James M. McPherson, *Battle Cry of Freedom*, 854 (1988).

an ontological difference—more than difference—between white and black. I have never observed this behavior with respect to other "races."

I do not mean to say that members of other racial groups have not had horrible experiences, even to the point of torture and genocide, for I am sure they have, especially Native Americans. But I myself do not see the same widespread emotional charge, the same intensity of feeling, on the part of white people with respect to the "race" of other groups. For example, so far as I am aware no other term of racial abuse has anything remotely like the force of the N-word.[17]

I can remember that in the fifties white people opposed to racial equality would commonly ask more liberal-minded whites, as a kind of clincher, how they would like it if their daughter were to "marry one." The idea was of course to show that the liberal white shared the racism of the overt racist, and should simply admit the fact and follow its logic, giving up his or her phony claims to moral superiority. This was something of an obsession in the white South. Today I never hear anyone ask that question, which would generally be regarded as unacceptable; but I think that if this barrier of manners were overcome, and you did ask how your white friends would feel if their child were to marry a Latino or Latina, an Asian American, a Native American, or an African American,

17. The reason, I think, is that the word does not merely express contempt or hatred; it is an exercise of racist power that recapitulates the experience of slavery itself. Compare what is so evil about the Nazis marching through Skokie: this is not merely an expression of hatred or revulsion, nor just the infliction of psychological or emotional harm in the form of forced recall of trauma, but a way of doing something, claiming the special and odious power of one who has successfully degraded another. For what the Nazis are saying is something like this: "Those with whom we identify—Hitler and his underlings—tortured and destroyed and gassed and killed your families and friends, and we are glad they did. If we had been there we would have done the same. We triumph in your degradation." You can say in response and perfectly rightly that the speakers are moral monsters, sadists, crazed, evil; but you cannot make a comparable claim of power over them. They are like the child-rapist and murderer who smirks at the parents of his victim in the courtroom, still affirming his pleasure in his crime and his immunity to any moral claims. To it there is no answer. Likewise, the N-word says: "Our people enslaved and degraded and tortured yours, and we are glad they did. We triumph in your degradation." It is a taunt to which there is no possible response.

To put it more generally, after Hitler's program of mass murder one cannot engage in anti-Semitic speech without affirming that crime and identifying with its perpetrators; likewise, one cannot use the N-word without affirming the crime it depends upon for its force, and identifying with its perpetrators.

my guess is that most would in fact have significantly more problematic emotional responses to the last possibility.

Or think of the phenomenon, known all over the country, called "white flight": this is I think almost invariably, and certainly in its most intense forms, a response specifically to African Americans buying houses in the neighborhood in question—and it is not only whites who move away. Or consider areas of the country where other forms of racism have predominated, like the southwest or northwest, but where blacks have more or less recently moved, and ask what the ladder of social hierarchy looks like; I think one would generally find African Americans at the bottom.

My own sense is that no one else has to face the same wall of feeling—doubt, hostility, contempt, fear—that black Americans face on a daily basis from their white fellow citizens. Faulkner captures what I mean as well as anyone when, in books like *Absalom! Absalom!* he expresses the kind of psychological torture the white mind inflicts upon itself, and others, as it tries to deny the full humanity of those it knows are fully human.[18]

In sum, I think this racial line is far more significant in the lives of white people than any other, and if that is true honesty requires us to recognize that fact.[19] To put it bluntly, I think that we whites are as a general matter much more racist in our attitudes towards blacks than

---

18. It is crucial to recognize that the history of black people includes not only legalized slavery but all the subsequent efforts to deny their humanity, especially those that we think of under the heading of Jim Crow, including lynching. On this see especially James Cone, *The Cross and the Lynching Tree* (2011), which in my view should be read by everyone in this country.

19. I know this is a difficult and somewhat controversial point, and that it does not help that the person who makes it is white. What do I know of the experience of the racial minorities in this country, after all, and who am I to speak to their circumstances? And suppose that African Americans as a group are worse off, socially and materially: exactly how should that matter to Vincent Chin, say, beaten to death by a pair of thugs for being Asian, or to the Mexican woman living with her children in a trailer on an isolated butte in Colorado, without schooling or medicine or anyone who speaks her language except the boss who employs her family, or the American Indian child, growing up without hope, without an economic future, on a reservation in South Dakota? Indeed how should it matter to the white family, barely surviving in desperate poverty in a West Virginia village, facing without help the diseases endemic to their condition?

This is a complex set of questions, to put it mildly. I think that no one in a country this rich should suffer the sort of poverty that millions do—and that they do is a national disgrace—and that it is also true that all of us, of all races, have a powerful interest in living

towards any other group, and that this shows up in our behavior and in the social structures we fashion and support. To this extent the white racists of the fifties were then—and still would be—pretty much right about the rest of us.

It is in these respects that I want to say that the experience of African Americans is unique. But it is true that the other forms of racial abuse and hatred are unique too, that is, that each group has its own characteristic experiences of abuse and contempt and injury. Take the obvious case of Native Americans, where there was real and widespread genocide, all over the country, both by public and private action. Which is worse,

---

in a world that is as free as possible from the evils of racist thought and feeling. In this connection, the violent and systematic subordination of blacks seems to me to have a special status in our country's life, past and present, and in our Constitution as well. To say this does not and should not mean blindness to other injustices.

For an account of the way in which white racism against blacks takes a physical toll on the body, see Sherman James's fascinating explanation of the severe difference between white and black hypertension, S.A. James, "John Henryism and the Health of African Americans," 18 *Culture, Medicine, and Psychiatry* 163–82 (1994). See also Rodney Clark *et al.*, "Racism as a Stressor for African Americans: A Biopsychosocial Model, October 1999 *American Psychologist* 805, and Chalmer E. Thompson and Helen A. Neville, "Racism, Mental Health, and Mental Health Practice," 27 *The Counselling Psychologist* 155 (1999). Especially interesting to one concerned with affirmative action in the university is Margaret A. Gibson and John U. Ogbu, *Minority Status and Schooling: A Comparative Study of Immigrant and Involuntary Minorities* (1991) which, as the subtitle suggests, argues that voluntary minorities—those who choose to come to this or another country—have a radically different experience from indigenous or involuntary minorities. The former have made a decision to move, they can remember the conditions from which they escaped, they can look forward to better times ahead, all of which are not available to a community that has experienced systematic and long-term oppression, especially by "race," which is a marker one cannot normally leave behind. On this scale African Americans are the ultimate involuntary minority, brought here by violence.

The conditions of Native Americans are comparable in important ways to those of blacks. The basic indicators of prosperity in these communities are for the most part extremely low—infant mortality, life expectancy, employment, income, alcoholism and other addictions, and political power. Indians are classic involuntary minorities, having been conquered by the immensely more powerful whites, made the object of genocide, and later treated shamefully. They are situated differently from blacks, however, in another way, which is that while there was a white war against them, in some sense a national war, there was no war *about* this war, no collective judgment that they had been treated unconscionably, and no constitutional amendments based upon that judgment. They do nonetheless have a special place in our constitutional tradition. Their story is a tragic one, and it calls for a response. Perhaps what we need is a national judgment, expressed in constitutional terms, specifically about this part of our shared history, about these members of the national polity.

slavery or genocide? One seeks to destroy human souls and to convert people into animals, the other seeks simply to kill them all, and it is hard to put these on an abstract scale of evil.[20]

So in saying that the black experience was unique, I am saying, what I think is true, that its form and its status in our history and in our law are different from others. It is the form of racism I have chosen to write about, in part because I simply do not know enough about Native American life and experience to begin to talk about it. In an important sense these two situations are not comparable, for there is no scale of relative awfulness on which they can be located.

All this does not mean that the fourteenth amendment does or should speak only to the relations between whites and blacks, or that affirmative action is proper only with respect to that group. Though I recognize that some of the arguments against affirmative action have force and validity, my own view is that the highly varied kind of affirmative action once practiced at my own and other universities was a right and good thing, and for a range of reasons: to compensate for past deprivation and discrimination, at both the individual and group level; to improve the quality of education for all students, and teachers too; and to help achieve a deep change in the ways in which we relate to one another across what we conceive of as racial lines. My point is not to put these practices into question, but to say that in the case of African Americans there is an additional and deeper justification, rooted both in the nature and intensity of white racism against blacks and in our constitutional history.

Stereotype vs. Malevolence

A second, somewhat different way, in which our language of "discrimination" misleads is this. In some forms, at least, it assumes that the evil against which it is directed is a kind of stereotyping, that is, a false as-

20. Are the purely material conditions of life in fact worse for blacks as a group than for any other group? This is in one sense an empirical question, and the answer to it would naturally to some degree depend upon the way conditions are measured—in terms of income, housing, safety, schooling, participation in government, and so on. But there is a sense in which no conditions are purely material: the question is what they mean in the lives of the people who face them. (Think of the voluntary poverty of a monk or nun, which is at least sometimes embraced with joy.) And the meaning of the conditions black people face is the work of the history to which I have been referring—the history and its present life in the minds of white people.

sumption that a particular individual has a set of social, personal, or physical characteristics in common with the larger group of which she is part—that she is good at math or basketball, or has a sense of rhythm or a hot temper. On this view the main vice of discrimination is that people are not judged accurately on their individual merits, but lumped with others with whom they do not belong. As an economist might say, discrimination is bad because it distorts the information flow and leads to defective market judgments in social and commercial relations.

This is indeed a bad thing but it is not the heart of white racism against blacks, which I think is not so much a matter of cognition or perception as of desire. Think of what we call Jim Crow laws, for example, prohibiting blacks from drinking at white water fountains, or sitting in white waiting rooms; or going to white schools. These laws did not rest on a mistaken lumping of the individual with his or her group, but had among their other aims a totally different reward for white people: the pleasure and satisfaction of treating other people like dirt, as less than you, less than human in fact, secure in the knowledge that as beings without rights they presented no legal, economic, or physical threat.[21] This kind of dehumanization is as base a desire as exists in human nature, but it does exist, potentially in all human beings, and it was present and active in the laws I describe; and I think it is often present and active in white responses to blacks today—including in the affirmative action debates, where it takes the form of superficial lament, but internal satisfaction, when "these people" prove themselves inferior once again.

The feelings I describe have vastly greater consequences than most

21. Charles S. Johnson, *Growing Up in the Black Belt*, 277–80 (1941), has a list of interracial taboos in certain southern counties that confirm this assessment, as does the famous account of race relations in Gunnar Myrdal, *An American Dilemma*, especially 610–15 (1944). Jim Crow was of course a complex phenomenon, trading on and stimulating the feelings I describe, and others too—like the sense that blacks were a source of contamination, with whom any intimacies were degrading for a white person—but also driven by domestic political interests, especially the desire of the established Democratic Party to consolidate its power by excluding the black voter. For this disturbing story, including the complicity of the federal judiciary, see J. Morgan Kousser, *The Shaping of Southern Politics: Suffrage Restrictions and the Establishment of the One-Party South, 1880–1910* (1974); the fine discussion of *Giles v. Harris*, 189 U.S. 475 (1903), and its background, in Richard Pildes, "Democracy, Anti-Democracy, and the Canon," 17 *Constitutional Commentary* 295 (2000); and the classic, C. Vann Woodward, *The Strange Career of Jim Crow*, (3d rev. ed. 1974). For a comparative study of postslavery regimes, see Frederick Cooper *et al.*, *Beyond Slavery* (2000).

of our talk recognizes. Think of the way in which issues relating to the "inner city" or welfare or schools or crime or public health are talked about in our media, in political debates, and so on: just barely beneath the surface of these conversations is the sense that what we are really talking about is black people, who are not fully people, fully entitled to what, in Ronald Dworkin's terms, is the equal respect and concern that is the linchpin of democracy.[22] We know this, for our government and society systematically fail to afford poor blacks the minimal conditions for a decent and healthy life. My own sense is that we would not tolerate living conditions like those of many urban blacks if the people in question were white;[23] and that we do tolerate terrible conditions for some whites in part because to address them seriously would require us to do the same for blacks, and this we will not do. This is not a matter of stereotyping but of dehumanization, in some sense deliberate dehumanization, to which we—those with power in our country—tend to be blind, in ourselves and in our neighbors, but which stands out as a shocking blot on our nation in the eyes of visitors.[24] The ghettoes of the north have to a large degree taken the place of the slave quarters of the south.

I also think that the line we maintain between white and black has the effect, and perhaps the purpose, of corroding or disabling our democracy, for it divides people where other interests would seem to unite them—interests in good public schools; in sensible penal policies and humane penal institutions; in rules concerning drugs and drug use that focus on education and rehabilitation not incarceration; in a decent

---

22. For a fine account of this phenomenon see Donald R. Kinder and Lynn Sanders, *Divided by Color: Racial Politics and Democratic Ideals* (1996), especially chapter five, "Subtle Prejudice for Modern Times." See also Thomas Holt, *The Problem of Race in the 21st Century* (2000) and the Gallup Poll fortuitously released as I was first working on this chapter (July 11, 2001), showing wide disparities in black and white perceptions of our common situation and attitudes towards it.

23. Look at the response to the opioid epidemic, which afflicts mainly whites and northern blacks, and which Congress has been reasonably happy to address.

24. We are so habituated to our own system of racism that it seems natural, until we are forced to see it with outside eyes, say those of visitors from abroad. Imagine this: you are a white person who becomes friends with a black African while working or studying in England; you suggest that he or she visit America, spending a few weeks traveling, then stay with you at your home for a couple of weeks. What would find yourself obliged to explain to your friend about your country, as he or she set off alone to travel in it?

public health system; in adequate transportation; in sensible controls on spreading suburbs; and so on. In every one of those issues, I believe, one can see at work the cancer of racism, and its effect is to distort democracy at the most basic level by preventing the formation of effective political majorities that would otherwise exist. Race may in this way be the cause — or a cause — of our remarkable public heartlessness as a nation, all the more surprising given our private generosity.

Abstract Judicial Language

A more familiar point is that the language of equal protection is disturbingly abstract in the terminology of its tests: "strict scrutiny," "compelling interest," "necessity," "suspect classification," etc. One can see some of what underlies this tendency, and it is in its own way good: the desire for neutral, abstract principles that will not commit the Court to the side of any litigant ahead of time.

The ideal is to create a kind of elegant intellectual structure that will decide cases in neutral and predictable ways, perhaps with a little adjustment from time to time by the Court, without requiring the Court to take sides in important political debates or struggles. The hope, that is, is that this part of constitutional law will become what people think of as real law, with the prestige and protection of universal categories and universal reason. At stake is the legitimacy of the Court itself, which depends upon its functioning as a legal and not a political agency, or so it is thought.[25]

But all this turns out to be something of a façade. Who after all is to decide what is a "suspect classification" or a "fundamental right" or a "compelling state interest," or whether a regulation is "necessary," and how are they to do so? These are not self-applying terms, and there is in the summary I have given, and I think in the opinions I have read, no coherent general articulation of purposes or values to which the Court could sensibly refer to give them definition. To think of this in the context of affirmative action cases, imagine yourself a judge asked to decide whether "racial diversity" offers educational benefits that rise to the level of a "compelling interest": how would you do this?

In practice, as is well known, the definition of these terms has fluc-

25. See Herbert Wechsler, "Toward Neutral Principles of Constitutional Law," 73 *Harvard Law Review* 1 (1959).

tuated, with the result that the law at the moment is not very far from the kind of interest-balancing that simply puts control of the question in the hands of the Court and gives up all but the pretense of the kind of control by reason and category that underlay the effort of abstraction in the first place.[26] My sense is that in the end the system that was meant to control and guide judicial discretion has to a large degree only masked it.

Likewise, the language most often used to justify affirmative action in education, that of "the educational benefits of diversity," seems to me at once too abstract and too anemic. It is not a marginal improvement in the quality of college education that is at stake, but the power of the state to address our gravest and deepest social evil in a sensible way. The proper goal is not simply diversity or variety or pluralism, whether of "race" or perspective or background, but a fundamental change in the ways in which African Americans in particular, but members of other races too, are imagined, indeed are encouraged to imagine themselves, and in the ways in which white Americans imagine themselves and their past too. The goal is not better education but social change at the deepest level; it is not a form of reparation, but a change in the practical and psychological structure of our national life, by the full incorporation of a whole group of people who have been systematically excluded and abused on the grounds of race.

The "Cost" to the White Student

Finally, and briefly, a word about an even narrower point, the common assumption that affirmative action necessarily works to the cost of the excluded white applicants who have better credentials. Think about the white high school senior, for example, who complains, in a way sensibly enough, that she has to worry about getting into a good college, while some of her black classmates, with lower grades and scores, have a better chance of making it. How would you respond to her?

Perhaps this way. Suppose, against the facts of history, that our fellow citizens of African descent had come here voluntarily and without the burdens of slavery; that they had been welcomed just as the Germans and English and Scots were, for example; and that they thus had had the

---

26. For an interesting analysis of the tendency of the Court to frame its decisions in formulas, see Robert F. Nagel, *Constitutional Cultures*, 121 (1989). Compare Alex Aleinikoff, "Constitutional Law in the Age of Balancing," 96 *Yale Law Journal* 943 (1987).

opportunity to become fully incorporated as equal citizens, with all that that means, from education to property; is it not possible that admission to college would be even more competitive for you than it is now?

The student's complaint, that is, rests on the assumption that the superiority in wealth, power, and culture that whites have enjoyed is the normal state of affairs, which affirmative action is threatening; not that the normal state of affairs would be actual equality between the races, which affirmative action is a small effort to attain.[27]

This is just a small instance in which it is plain that, however opposed he or she may be to racial discrimination, every white person is in some sense—in terms of power, self-image, the right to claim no race at all—its beneficiary. This is of course profoundly distasteful, but it is true, and in our efforts to talk about this matter we should try to reflect that truth.[28]

How Should We Think about Race?

If I have captured something of the way we talk about race in the law, especially in connection with affirmative action, and something too of what is wrong with it, can we find a way to do better? Is there any other way, in particular, in which we might think about an affirmative action case, say one involving the use of racial categories by a state university in

27. Some people feel resentful of public efforts to redress racial injustice on the grounds that their ancestors came long after slavery was over and that they and their families have not only not practiced racial discrimination, they have been consistently opposed to it. "Let the descendants of slaveowners pay, perhaps, but not us, who have done nothing." There are several difficulties with this position, the most obvious perhaps the one made in the next paragraph of the text, that all white people are in fact privileged by our racial system, even if they do not wish to be. Being white in America is like living in a house that was built by slaves before the Civil War.

It is also true that slavery was not so long ago. My own great aunt, whom I remember meeting, was born in 1860, and I have myself known people whose parents and grandparents were born into slavery. Equally important, overt and legalized disenfranchisement of black people continued until the Voting Rights Act of 1965, and there is evidence that it is going on today in a more covert way.

28. Is it in fact possible that the very commitment to abstraction that characterizes legal discourse in this field, its search for neutral categories, its erasure of what is historically and constitutionally special about the situation of black Americans, is driven without our knowing it by the hidden desires of racism? Compare Robert M. Cover, *Justice Accused: Antislavery and the Judicial Process* (1975).

the admission process to ensure the presence of African Americans in the student body? (I shall assume for the moment that the program reaches only African Americans, not members of other races.)

Civil War Amendments

The first step might be to think of the Civil War amendments less as an effort to create neutral and universal rules of law, to be applied by the work of a universal reason—as is perhaps true of the Bill of Rights—than as an effort to address the greatest single social and political issue the nation has ever faced, human slavery and its consequences, including the denial of full citizenship to the descendants of slaves. It is obvious that the Framers saw this as a long process—hence the use of the constitutional amendment as a way to deal with it—and that they anticipated serious and systematic state hostility to the newly freed slaves, for it is against this danger that the amendments were meant to guard. The amendments were in large part aimed at preventing the states from interfering with the process by which newly freed blacks, or those freed earlier, could become integrated into the nation as full citizens, autonomous, capable, independent.[29] This is a way of thinking of the amendments as meant to achieve something specific in the world, not just as articulations of general political or philosophic principles to be applied to all alike.

From this perspective it would be simply bizarre to use the fourteenth amendment to strike down reasonable state efforts to help African Americans achieve full autonomy and integration. The states would be doing just what the amendments wanted them to do—instead of the particularly odious kind of group warfare they had waged against African Americans for centuries, which many of them were in fact to continue to wage, in different guises, for another century at least. "Discrimination"—which sounds like a neutral term defining a generalized evil—in fact means something very different indeed when it refers to action by the white majority to increase their domination over blacks and when it

29. Indeed, the equal protection language could be read to require more: affirmative action, in fact, to protect blacks against lawlessness and violence at the hands of whites. See Robin West, *Progressive Constitutionalism: Reconstructing the Fourteenth Amendment* (1994), especially her excellent chapter one, "Toward an Abolitionist Interpretation of the Fourteenth Amendment."

refers to action by the same majority designed to reduce it.[30] Black people have been subjected to sustained private and public dehumanization, which can hardly be said of the white student who is not able to get into the college of his or her choice.

I am suggesting, that is, that we might think of this set of amendments as being far more "result-oriented" than we usually do, as aimed less at the articulation of a general principle by which to test all state legislation than at the specific result of trying to help black Americans get on their feet and flourish in a world in which they faced constant racial opposition.[31] This view is all the more compelling, to me at least,

---

30. See Richard Lempert, "The Force of Irony: On the Morality of Affirmative Action and *United Steelworkers v. Weber*," 95 *Ethics* 85 (1984), and my discussion of *Weber* in *Justice as Translation*, 218–22 (1990).

31. *The Slaughterhouse Cases*, 83 U.S. (16 Wall.) 36 (1872), in other respects objectionable, could provide a starting point, for the Court here held that the fourteenth amendment was to be read not as a general grant of power to review the reasonableness or propriety of state legislation, but as directed to the plight of freed blacks. See my brief discussion in "Reading Texts, Reading Traditions: African Masks and American Law," 12 *Yale Journal of Law and the Humanities* 117, 125–26 (2000).

This view was reiterated in *Strauder v. West Virginia*, 100 U.S. 303 (1880), where the Court said its purpose was "to assure to the colored race the enjoyment of all the civil rights that under the law are enjoyed by white persons, and to give to that race the protection of the general government, in that enjoyment, whenever it should be denied by the States."

The obvious counter to my position is (1) that the Framers of the fourteenth amendment did not in fact compose that text in terms of race or slavery, let alone identify the specific condition of black Americans, and (2) that it would have been worse, for blacks and everyone else, had they done so, for a group-specific protection in a Constitution otherwise largely part cast in universalist terms would be likely to increase rather than reduce racial hostility.

Of course it is a real question how the Framers' choice of general language is to be read, but I do not think that it precludes the reading I propose. There can be no question that it is the situation of blacks to which the fourteenth amendment is mainly directed, especially when it is read in connection with the thirteenth and fifteenth. And to say that the paradigm the Framers have in mind should be treated with particular respect and solicitude in no way undermines their wish to articulate a standard that would reach other cases as well—just as in reading the fourth amendment it would be right to give scrupulous though not exclusive attention to cases that are especially close to the writs of assistance that were the Framers' paradigm for improper governmental searches. (But see *Almeida-Sanchez v. United States*, 413 U.S. 266 [1973]) My view is not that the fourteenth amendment should reach no other cases, no other people, but only to say that the special case of African Americans ought to be treated as the paradigm it actually was.

The second half of the argument given above I think actually reinforces my reading. Of course one would not want a constitutional amendment framed in terms of one racial

when we consider the disgraceful period of Jim Crow and the Court's shameful complicity in it, during which the conditions against which the amendments were addressed were to a large degree continued under the force of law, including legalized disenfranchisement.[32] Given this history the Court ought to be extremely deferential to any sincere state effort to achieve, rather than frustrate, the purposes of the amendments.

"State Action"

I also think we should re-examine the "state action" doctrine. This is the rule that the Constitution reaches discrimination only at the hands of the state, or one of its agents or subdivisions, not of private parties.

In the affirmative action cases the issue arises this way: the Court has agreed that a state agency, such as a university, may use racial classifications to counter the effects of its own prior unconstitutional racial discrimination (this would, that is, be a "compelling interest"); on the other hand, it may not act in this way to counter the effects of discrimination by other states, or other branches of its own state, and certainly not to counter the effects of what is termed "societal discrimination." There are two arguments at work here: first that private discrimination would have been beyond the reach of the fourteenth amendment when it occurred and cannot thus justify ameliorative action today; and second that societal discrimination is in any event too amorphous and uncertain to work as an appropriate standard for legislative action.

The view that the Constitution reaches only state action rests on one

---

group, and for both the reasons suggested. But that very fact is one reason why the Framers might have composed a universalist text not out of universalist impulses but in response to the dangers and evils of a particular situation. I think it would be much closer to the meaning of this text in its context to read it as especially focused on the circumstances of blacks than to read it, as the Court now seems to, as a wholly neutral prohibition of the use of racial classifications, without distinguishing the case in which those classifications are used to perpetuate the racial domination against which the amendment is directed from the case in which they are used to erode it.

32. See especially *Giles v. Harris*, 189 U.S. 475 (1903), explained and analyzed well in R. Pildes, "Democracy, Anti-Democracy and the Canon," 17 *Constitutional Commentary* 295 (2000). For a general history see the well-known book by C. Vann Woodward, *The Strange Career of Jim Crow* (rev. ed. 1966). Like Thomas Holt in *The Problem of Race in the 21st Century* (2000), Woodward shows that in race relations as all else there are significant changes over time, some of them dramatic. But in the accounts of both writers, there is a deep theme of persistent white racial hostility, sometimes simmering, sometimes on the boil, but always present.

great textual pillar, the fact that the fourteenth amendment begins with the language, "no state shall . . ." and goes on to specify various things, including "deny any person equal protection of the laws." It is supported as well by the nature of the Constitution more generally, which is of course meant to define and limit the powers of government, not to promulgate general rules of law. And it is evident that the purpose of the fourteenth amendment at a general level was to subject the state's treatment of the individual person to substantial constitutional control, which before was not the case—indeed it could not have been, if the compromise the Framers originally drew on slavery, permitting but not mentioning it, were to survive. All this amounts to a strong argument for the state action requirement.

But it is not completely unanswerable, especially where, as here, the question arises at one remove: the question is not whether the societal discrimination the state wishes to redress was itself a violation of the fourteenth amendment, but whether its private or societal character disqualifies it as a justification the state may now invoke to support its remedial policies.

Think here of the state action question in perhaps its purest form, in connection with the series of "sit-in" cases in the early 1960s. The facts were typically something like this: black activists, or black activists and their white supporters together, would enter a restaurant or store or other such establishment to request service against the insistence by the management that they would serve only white customers. They would be asked to leave and refuse. Usually they would be prosecuted under a statute or ordinance that was not cast in racial terms but simply made it a crime to enter property, or to remain on it, against the expressed will of the owner.

The question was whether the convictions violated the fourteenth amendment; the obvious argument was that they did not, for the state was not the source of the decision to discriminate. On this view exclusion was a purely private judgment, enforced in a neutral way by the state, which claimed that it would have acted equally energetically on behalf of a black restauranteur who wished to exclude white customers. The state would in fact have had not the slightest objection, it was said, if an owner of a restaurant wanted his establishment to be open to people of both races, or only to integrated groups. A decision for the protesters, it was argued, would threaten the right of the people to make free choices in the most private aspects of their lives, at parties given in their own homes for example, or in the choice of rooming house boarders.

As is well known, the Court found technical ways to reverse the convictions without directly facing the state action question, in this way putting pressure on Congress to deal with the issue, which it did in the 1964 Civil Rights Act. This statute was premised mainly on the commerce power of the Congress, rather than the fourteenth amendment, and therefore no substantial state action question was presented. The new antidiscrimination law was conceptualized, that is, not as the reversal of a state policy on race but simply as the regulation of a certain part of the economy, which under the expansive readings of the commerce power in the New Deal cases was practically the entire thing.

But suppose that Congress had not acted. Is it obvious that these convictions were beyond the reach of the fourteenth amendment? An argument that they were not could begin with the fact that the line between state and private action, especially in connection with racial discrimination, is by no means as clear as the doctrine suggests. First, consider the fact that in many of the southern states, for example, and some of the northern ones, every act of so-called private discrimination occurring during the first half of the twentieth century would have had the support of official declarations from every branch of the state government—executive, legislative, and judicial.[33] When a state says that its policy is to segregate the races in every feasible way,[34] in what sense are private acts that are consistent with this policy merely private acts? It is impossible for me to believe that the governmental policies and declarations would not have a substantial reinforcing, perhaps guiding, effect. One task and hope of the law is to shape culture, and that means to reach private action; when the law deliberately reinforces a racist culture it may perhaps be held accountable for conduct beyond that which it specifically requires or prohibits. The fact that in the sit-in case there is no

33. See, *e.g.*, the summary of Louisiana law in *Garner v. Louisiana*, 368 U.S. 157, 178–81 (Douglas, J., concurring).

34. For one judicial statement of the policy of racial subordination see *Naim v. Naim*, 87 S.E.2d 749 (Va. 1955): "We are unable to read in the Fourteenth Amendment to the Constitution, or in any other provision of that great document, any words or any intendment which prohibit the State from enacting legislation to preserve the racial integrity of its citizens, or which denies the power of the State to regulate the marriage relation so that it will not have a mongrel breed of citizens. We find there no requirement that the State shall

state policy enforcing segregation in lunchrooms, for example, would hardly undo the effect on all the persons involved of the state's bold and unrelenting commitment to the principle of black inferiority and the separation of the races.

Justice Douglas

A more radical way to connect the state with "private" action was suggested by Justice Douglas in the sit-in cases, when he said that custom could be law and hence "state action" for purposes of the fourteenth amendment.[35] I think his idea was that when one group, in this case whites motivated by racial animosity towards blacks, have such a practical monopoly of private and public power that they may simply choose whether to achieve their objectives through the arms of the state or through concerted private action it ought not matter which form of power they elect to use. In other words, when a group is so dominant that it can use the agencies of the state if it chooses, its extra-governmental actions ought not be immune from all constitutional consideration simply because it chose to act "privately."[36]

In support of Justice Douglas's approach consider the fact that slavery was in its origins to a large degree private not public. It emerged as a private practice, mainly in the southern states, presumably with the ap-

---

not legislate to prevent the obliteration of racial pride, but must permit the corruption of blood even though it weaken or destroy the quality of its citizenship."

35. See *Garner v. Louisiana*, 368 U.S. 157, at 179–81 (1961), and Justice Marshall's dissenting opinion in *Jackson v. Metropolitan Edison*, 419 U.S. 345, 365 (1974). A more familiar argument focused on the character of restaurants, hotels, lunchrooms, and the like, as businesses "affected with a public interest." Under ancient common law they had an obligation to serve all people and at fair prices. Of course, the fact that the common law has this principle does not mean that it is automatically a principle of our constitutional law, but Douglas used it to provide a language, a set of instances and ideas, by which the fourteenth amendment could reach some "private" judgments to discriminate without reaching all—the lunchroom but not the social club. When one adds the fact that these facilities are heavily regulated by the state, the argument that they are quasi-public becomes still stronger. On the other hand, this way of thinking would seem to make the restaurants or other businesses "state actors" for all purposes, meaning that other provisions of the Constitution would apply to them—for example the establishment clause, which would arguably make it unconstitutional for the restaurant owner to display a religious symbol or text on the wall of his or her restaurant.

36. Reasoning like this was also at work in *Terry v. Adams*, 345 U.S. 461 (1953), which held that "private" political primaries were subject to constitutional limitations (though

proval of those with power in the community; only once established did it become legalized, through legislative and judicial action. Indeed, the most comprehensive and draconian slave codes were not promulgated until the middle years of the nineteenth century, almost 200 years after the beginning. Slavery was a product of the common law, a legalization of social practice, a fact that lends support to the idea that the social practices that are its progeny might be within the ambit of the Constitution. A fusion of the private and the public is built into the history of slavery and racial discrimination alike.

This is recognized in the Constitution itself, for the thirteenth amendment, prohibiting slavery, has no state action language at all, but simply says:

> Neither slavery nor involuntary servitude, except as a punishment for crime whereof the party shall have been duly convicted, shall exist within the United States, or any place subject to their jurisdiction.

This amendment makes human slavery the proper object of federal concern even if it receives no support whatever from agencies of the state. A federal statute accordingly makes it a crime to treat another person as a slave, without any requirement that the state (or federal) government in any way support or involve itself in that slavery.[37] When one recognizes that the sorts of discrimination and abuse to which the descendants of

---

that case could presumably be limited to instances where the supposedly private parties were carrying out public functions). One could also invoke here by analogy the arguments against excessive formalism in corporate law made by Nina Mendelson, "A Control-Based Approach to Shareholder Liability," 102 *Columbia Law Review* 1203 (2002).

Unlike the "affected with a public interest" rationale, Douglas's second approach to what is involved when a private business acts to maintain white domination over blacks would not make those businesses state actors for all purposes, but only when they are acting to reinforce the evil against which the amendment is directed. In this sense it is another move away from abstraction to address the particularity of our situation. This is all an argument for the rejection of the now-standard way of thinking about "state action"—namely by the degree of "entwinement" between the "state" and the "private actor"—whenever the issue is the perpetuation of white domination of blacks. For a more recent case, see *Brentwood Academy v. Tennessee Secondary School Athletic Ass'n*, 531 U.S. 288 (2001).

Of course others have also argued against the state action doctrine, *e.g.*, Robin West in *Progressive Constitutionalism*, 34, 110–11, 117–20.

37. 18 U.S.C.A. 77, § 1584: "Whoever knowingly and willfully holds to involuntary servitude or sells into any condition of involuntary servitude, any other person for any term,

slaves in this country have been regularly subjected are, as a cultural and factual matter, an effort to maintain the view of the world that underlay slavery—to perpetuate it in another form—it may not be as much of a stretch as first appears to hold that the Constitution speaks to systematic racism in the private as well as the public sector—or, to use the language of *Plessy v. Ferguson*,[38] that it aims at "social" as well as "political" equality.

This argument has special force wherever agencies of the state have in the past supported racism, and it is even more plausible where—as is true in affirmative action cases—the question is not whether "private conduct or "societal discrimination" is itself subject to judicial regulation under the Constitution but only whether a state may constitutionally base remedial action upon it, as a legacy of the slavery against which the amendments are specifically directed.[39] In this context the second argument mentioned above, that societal discrimination is too amorphous to serve as a ground for state action, seems very weak. Insofar as the states are themselves trying in a genuine and rational way to address the problem of radical injustice to which the amendments were themselves directed, their efforts should be applauded and supported by the Court, and the rest of us, not undermined.

Which Race?

One of the difficulties faced by those who defend affirmative action programs is that of explaining exactly why one racial or ethnic group is included, another excluded. The trial judge in the University of Michigan Law School case said, for example, that the School had no principled way of explaining why it singled out African Americans, Mexican Americans, Native Americans, and Puerto Ricans raised on the U.S. mainland. "Certainly, other groups have also been subjected to discrimination, such as Arabs and southern and eastern Europeans, to name but a few . . ."[40] If the idea is to remedy past discrimination that has resulted in under-

---

or brings within the United States any person so held, shall be fined under this title or imprisoned not more than 20 years, or both."

38. 163 U.S. 537 (1896).

39. As Justice Douglas told the story briefly in *Bell v. Maryland*, "The Black Codes were a substitute for slavery; segregation was a substitute for the Black Codes; the discrimination in these sit-in cases is a relic of slavery." 378 U.S. 247–48 (1964).

40. *Grutter v. Bollinger*, 137 F. Supp.2d 821, 852 (E.D.Mich 2001).

representation in the legal profession, as some programs put it,[41] Polish people would certainly seem to have a claim. And why only Latinos and Latinas who are Mexican in origin? Why only mainland-raised Puerto Ricans? And how about Asian Americans, a category that includes an enormous diversity with respect both to prior national and cultural background and to present economic and social status?

The language of "diversity," as I said above, seems simply too weak to deal with the imperatives presented by the special circumstances of African Americans and it leads to distinctions that are hard to explain or defend. My own sense is that affirmative action programs, in some sense originally based on special moral and political claims of blacks, have been extended in a way that both makes them harder to explain and justify and ends up diluting and obscuring the claims of blacks themselves.

How should we think about affirmative action, then? I think a line can be drawn distinguishing between African Americans and all others, for the reasons I have been setting forth from the beginning of this chapter, and that rather than strict scrutiny, a very high degree of judicial deference should be paid to sensible and responsible attempts by the state to address what is in my view the most serious of all our social and moral problems. This would include not only the judgment to admit African Americans who would not, on other criteria, be admitted to universities, but also a decision to spend time and money to help them to succeed there.

As for other groups, the rationale of diversity, supported by the desire to redress prior and present patterns of discrimination, does make sense to me. Without the special case of African Americans, such a program could be far less race-dependent than it now is, far more focused on the particular experience and situation of individual applicants. If diversity of background and experience and outlook is the goal, and I think it is a fine one, then a university ought to be interested on these grounds in a blue collar white man, a fundamentalist Christian woman, a Hasidic Jew, a Sikh or Hindu, a man or woman from the barrio in Los Angeles, a farm worker's child, a person who grew up as the only Asian American in her town in Georgia, a woman who worked during college in a pregnancy

---

41. See, for example, the University of Colorado Law School program, quoted in *The Legal Imagination*, 392–93.

clinic in southeast Washington, an Ojibwe man from the White Earth reservation in Minnesota, and so on.

The burdens or handicaps faced by any of these people should be relevant to their admission, including those based upon the fact that others regard them as belonging to a "race" different from the "white race." And if a state, or its universities, did conclude that the circumstances of some other race made claims as a group comparable to those of blacks—based on past or present deprivation, discrimination, or oppression—I think the courts should give considerable weight to such a determination too.

All of this could be done far more honestly and intelligibly, if the special core case of the African Americans were recognized as distinctive and treated accordingly. The approach to diversity I suggest might attract less hostility than the kind of program we now have, both from the courts and from segments of the public, for the diversity program would not be seen to be about "race" in the same sense that a program involving African Americans would.[42]

Obviously I support affirmative action on the merits, especially for blacks. But I should stress that the two shifts in doctrine I have suggested—(1) reading the fourteenth amendment as focusing especially on protecting blacks against the hostility of whites and (2) proposing a revision of the state action doctrine along the lines suggested by Justice Douglas—would not result in a constitutional *obligation* that the states adopt affirmative action programs in university or other contexts.

These programs are on the merits highly controversial and contested, and while I am strongly disposed to favor them, I also recognize that rational—if in my view erroneous—arguments can be made against them, cast in terms of fairness to white applicants, the importance of neutral standards of intellectual achievement and capacity, the claim of damage done to the intended beneficiaries of the program, or the improper omission of whites who have suffered economic and other forms of deprivation.

My point is here very different, having to do with the attitude the Supreme Court, and lower courts too, should take towards a state agency that has considered these matters, heard arguments both ways, and come

42. If I am right, this supports my sense that this group has a "race" as no other group in our country does.

to the conclusion that such a program is a wise and good thing. Given the aims of the fourteenth amendment and the shameful history of the nation—including state and federal courts—since that time, I think the Court has no business "strictly scrutinizing" reasonable state efforts to advance the purposes of the Civil War amendments, but should instead be glad that the state has assumed the kind of responsibility it has and defer to its rational judgments.

Race—and by this I mean the socially defined line between whites and blacks—is the ultimate taken-for-granted of our culture; we maintain it, both in our official and in our unofficial behavior, as I in fact have been doing throughout this article. It is a continuing badge of slavery. So long as it exists, the Court should display, at the very least, a tolerant attitude towards state efforts to end the evils it has produced.

The "Fact" of "Race"

I want to make one more point, which brings us back to *Huckleberry Finn* and its implication of the white reader in the racism that is its subject. Built into the argument at every stage so far is the belief that people are in fact of different races. Everyone "knows" that whites are one thing, blacks another. Intermarriage is of course possible, but again, everyone knows that the child of such a marriage is black, not white. Yet it is perfectly plain that race is not a natural or biological fact.[43] Surely the social rule regarding children of mixed marriages, that they are "black" not "white," is a demonstration that it is an arbitrary social and legal construct; a system of racism could with equal plausibility hold the opposite, that one drop of the blood of the master race entitles a person to all the privileges of that status. Many of the physical features we associate with "race," such as skin color and facial features, are inherited separately, not as a package. And similarity in skin color may in fact not represent a common ancestry, but a parallel adaptation on the part of distant populations.

If you turn to genetic studies of race, you find that the people of Africa have greater genetic variation than other populations—think of the towering and thin Masai compared to the short pygmies, for example, or the enormous variation in head shape and facial features among Afri-

43. For a good introduction to this issue, see Stephan Molnar, *Human Variation, Races, Types, and Ethnic Groups* (6th ed. 2006).

cans. This makes it exceedingly odd to think of the people of Africa[44] as a single race. But those of us who are western whites tend not to see these differences, or not to see them clearly, because in our minds they are less significant than the single criterion of skin color. This is what it means to have a mind shaped by the ideology of race: to think that the differences we choose to observe and act on are real and natural.

The Language of War

Finally I wish to draw attention to another feature of the language of race, and a source of its power, namely that it creates a connection, a web of identity and responsibility in fact, between people who have not chosen each other, and are not related by blood or marriage. Thus when a black man steals or rapes or kills, white people often tend to look to black people, or at least black men, in a demanding or at least questioning way: "What have you to say about that? You people are . . ." But by what warrant do we whites do that? The person we implicitly address, or hold responsible, has no more real relation with the criminal than we do. Think how differently gender works. I suppose a vast majority of violent crimes are committed by males, but it is not common to see the acts of one male attributed to all. That is, our culture does not draw among men the kind of connection that it regularly draws among those defined by race, especially African Americans.

The language of race in this context, white against black, works like the language of war. Its logic is the same as that by which a nation at war holds all of the people they think of as the enemy responsible for what any of them does. "These people are . . . " In the case of war, this feature of the language has a dreadful purpose, which is to enable us to deny the humanity that unites us with the people on the other side, a denial that is necessary for war to go on at all. It is what enables a person to drop incendiary bombs on Tokyo or Dresden or London or Baghdad. The psychological cost of this denial is enormous, for it is obviously false, but, as I say, it is necessary to the existence of war, to which we must look for any justification.

---

44. In fact one study shows that Africans as a group are more genetically diverse than all the inhabitants of the rest of the world combined. Michael C. Campbell and Sarah A. Tishkoff, "African Genetic Diversity," 9 *Annual Review of Genomics and Genetics* 403–433 (2008).

That our language of race works like a language of war is no accident, since its origins were as a language of war, a language that would justify the war of whites against blacks—their seizure, sale, and total subjugation, by torture and murder if necessary.

This may explain a feeling I have had about *Brown v. Board of Education*,[45] that it was a victory like a martial victory, a triumph over an enemy—and hence that it was entirely beside the point to agonize about whether it treated with appropriate "neutrality" the conflict between the white desire for segregation and the black desire for integration.[46] There is a real sense in which the Civil War did not end at Appomattox, but continued, with African Americans as its continued victims, at least for another century, and in many ways continues at the present moment. As a white northerner in the fifties I can remember feeling with great righteousness, and erroneously, that the evil against which *Brown* was directed was specifically and exclusively a southern one, a remnant of the war in fact. In those days "Yankee" and "Rebel" were still terms of ordinary speech, and I think my own feelings about *Brown*, though I only recognized this recently, were those of victory, victory in a war—one that would require further action, of course, for the war was not yet entirely won, but a decisive victory nonetheless.

It also explains something else, for me at least. I was raised to believe that the language of race always drew lines among human beings that ought never to be drawn. The inference I drew was that race is a topic on which one should never speak. To refer to another person's race in their presence was an ultimate rudeness; to do so in their absence a kind of dishonesty. When the issue of affirmative action first arose in my life, very early in my teaching years at the University of Colorado, I argued strenuously that it ought to be race-neutral, and that it should speak instead of hardship, deprivation, oppression, on the view that these were ultimately individual matters. I think what I was seeing, without quite knowing it, was that the language of race was the language of war, and I thought it should never be used. But I now think this was and is an impossible principle: race is in fact created by our society, and given meaning, and we cannot deny this. We have to use the language, bad as it is.

45. 347 U.S. 483 (1954)

46. See Wechsler, "Toward Neutral Principles of Constitutional Law," 73 *Harvard Law Review* 1 (1959).

The days of *Brown*, and the early days of affirmative action too, were days of innocence. We can now begin to see, including even northerners like me, what Lincoln told us in his Second Inaugural, that this was and is one nation, with one history and one great defining national "offense," to use his and the Bible's word, in which all white people and the state itself are implicated. The true story is that the evil of racial thought is not southern but national, and the battle of today is not between regions but within our hearts.

Yet all this suggests that the nomenclature of the Civil War amendments has more relevance than is commonly recognized, not only as a matter of the context in which they were promulgated and adopted; they speak to a civil war that still rages in our society, in our schools, in ourselves, and they should be so interpreted. I think it is the right, the only, thing for the Court to do, to recognize that white racism is the continuation of a war against our fellow citizens, defined by "race," and that as an evil of this kind it calls for responses that rest on the great purposes of the Civil War itself and the amendments it made possible, certainly to the extent of adopting an attitude of respect and deference, indeed thankfulness, towards every reasonable effort of the state to bring that war to an end.

When Mark Twain finds himself imagining more and more fully the relation between Huck and Jim as a relation between human beings—a relation of love and redemption, in fact, for Jim saves Huck not only pragmatically but psychologically—he brings simultaneously into the circle of attention the simultaneous moral impossibility of racial thought and its unavoidability. We are now in truth situated much as he was then. There is no easy way to imagine ourselves out of the world of deep and violent injustice we have created, and that we recreate every day. But that is our task, and we shall have a much better chance of doing something right and valuable if we can find ways of talking and thinking, ways of telling our national story, that do justice to its meaning.

This chapter has told the story of one kind of inequality, racial inequality, which the law has to some degree tried to correct, with some real success—think of *Brown v. Board of Education*—but in other respects has failed miserably. The promise of the Civil War amendments, of Martin Luther King, of *Brown* itself, has never been kept. This chapter has been an effort, necessarily incomplete, to suggest how we might keep more of that promise than we have so far managed to do, on behalf not only of those who have suffered at our hands but of the nation itself and its Constitution.

The issues raised here have become much more visible in recent years in our shared life. White supremacists are again a public part of our social and political life, and the fear and hatred that drive them has been stimulated and encouraged at the highest levels. It is clear I think to almost everyone that racial animosity is no longer reducible to improper judgments of fact in the form of racial stereotypes, but rests on its own malevolence. While what I say about the special place of black Americans in this drama is I think true, it is also more obvious to me than it once was that somewhat similar animosities are directed at others, especially Latinos and Latinas, Native Americans, and Muslims as well. We face a deliberate political program of dehumanization that insists on the legitimacy of racial and ethnic contempt, hatred, and violence.

Does this change in context make what I say here simply a relic of a gentler and more reasonable age? Or is there something to be learned about race and about how the law treats it, and should treat it, from what I said? I mean this as a real question.

If we think of law as in part a system of authorities, to be identified, defined, and interpreted, singly and together, you might want to ask: What authorities do I identify in this chapter, and how do I define and interpret them? What is your judgment about what I do? If the heart of law lies in a set of responsibilities and practices, how does what I say here define them? Do I live up to them?

It will not have escaped you that in this chapter there are many footnotes, many of them long, presenting questions or elaborating arguments, one way or another. Are they important? What would the chapter be like if they, or most of them, had been omitted? Is there something here that is important to what we mean by legal thinking?

As I have suggested, in reading this chapter you engage in a conversation with it. Can you characterize that conversation? Can you evaluate it? What does it mean to the world that such conversations go on, or do not do so?

I said earlier that Holmes's achievement in the two opinions we read was one of character and identity. What character and identity do you see in me, as the writer of this chapter? In you, as its critic?

Finally, what does it mean, for the law, and for the world we live in, that someone like me, or you, can write a piece like this chapter, however misguided it may seem to be to someone else?

4

Tensions Defining the Art of Law

In this chapter I elaborate the idea expressed in the last three, that law is at heart not just a system or scheme of rules, as we often think of it; nor is it simply a set of institutional arrangements that can be adequately described in a language of social science; rather, it is an inherently unstable structure of thought and expression, built upon a distinct set of dynamic and dialogic tensions. Of course the law has rules, as we have seen in the Model Penal Code, and they are important. But alone they do not achieve much. They need to be read and acted upon, made the material of the activity I call the art of law.

Law is a form of life that must work with the rules and other materials of law, but is not reducible to them. It has the value of justice at its heart. It is a process, built upon a set of internal tensions, by which the old is made new, over and over again.

You may remember in particular the discussion of tensions at work in the construction and use of the Model Penal Code: tensions among the stated purposes of the criminal law, tensions between the Code and common law, tensions between the Code and constitutional law, tensions between the trial of guilt, regulated by substantive criminal law, and the other stages of the criminal process, including police behavior, the exercise of prosecutorial discretion, judicial sentencing, and the management of prisons and parole. As I said, these tensions call upon the lawyer and judge to exercise an art of language, an art of writing, by which they may be addressed.

Here I expand on what I said there by focusing on a similar but more basic set of tensions, present in law more generally, tensions that do much to define our law and the way it works. My idea is in this way to render more explicit than I have so far done the vision of law itself out of which I have been functioning, as an art of language, of thought and expression, as the art of using law's language well.

As you read it, I urge you once again to think not only about what is said in this chapter but also about the nature of your own responses to it. How important is it to the world, if at all, that the view of law expressed here he widely accepted, by judges, by legislators, by teachers, indeed by citizens? That the kind of conversation in which you are engaging here continue to take place?

I HAVE SUGGESTED THAT THE ART OF LAW can be seen as an art of language. But what do I mean by language?

Law as Language

When I was an undergraduate I studied Greek, and found myself asking questions like the following: How is this language put together? What are its key terms of value, of social and natural description, of psychology, and what do they mean? What are its principles of grammar and syntax, governing the way in which sentences can be composed? What are the forms of thought and imagination that this language invites and made possible? What, in short, can be said and done in this language that cannot be said and done in English?

When I came to law school I felt that in learning law I was also learning a new language.

It was like learning Greek, except that it was a language in which to think about and debate important contemporary questions of our shared existence. I was learning it for use in the world, the world of law and power, rather than as a way of engaging with literary and philosophic texts. That is, for me learning the language of the law was not an academic or purely intellectual activity, but training in a profession that I intended to practice.

I thought of this future most readily in small-town-lawyer terms: I could imagine a client coming in off the street with a problem—a sense of threat or frustration or loss—that he or she could not handle without help. Law was the language into which this problem would have to be translated: it was the language I would use to define the problem and to make sense of it, and to think about its larger context too. It would ultimately be a language of power, producing a result authorized and enforced by the government.

The questions I had for it were much the same as those I had about Greek. How is this language put together? What are its key terms of value, of social and natural description, of psychology, and what do they mean? What are the principles that govern the way in which its sentences can be composed? What are the forms of thought and imagination, the kinds of reasoning, that this language invites and made possible? What, in short, can be said and done in this language that cannot be said and done in ordinary English? And: what will it mean for me to give myself the mind and character of a lawyer, as one who speaks this language?

As I imagined it, in law practice I would be talking about what really mattered, in competition and cooperation with others who were doing likewise, before judges who were also talking about what really mattered.

For what we were talking about was important not only to our clients, which it surely was—would they be compensated for their injury, or hold on to their land, or lose their inheritance?—but to the world: and this not so much because the outcome of the particular case mattered, but because it always matters very much to the world how such cases are debated and resolved. Every case performs an answer to the question: What are our institutions of justice? How well—how justly—do they work? How should they work? And nothing is more important to a healthy community than justice.

I saw the law as a wonderful system in which power worked through conversation, through open argument and persuasion. In principle at least, everyone got his or her opportunity to present the case in the best way possible, and to answer what was said on the other side. In a legal hearing one could say whatever it was necessary or crucial to say about this injury, this divorce, this failed agreement, this event in the real world.[1]

---

1. If a case was to be settled by negotiation, the hearing still remained the model of legal expression, because at every stage the lawyers were imagining that the case would proceed to trial and thinking ahead of time of the arguments that would be made both ways. Even

To engage in this complex activity it was crucial that I should be able to learn to read and speak and write the language of the law, and do it well, in two senses: that I should be an effective counselor and advocate; and that in doing so I should be able to conceive of myself as doing something of value not only to my client but to the world—contributing to the maintenance of our institutions of justice, indeed contributing to the realization of justice itself.

Of course, as in all language use, I could see that the conversation of the law would always be imperfect: there would always be something left out, something out of tune, something stuck in, always a deep imperfection. Sometimes I thought that the legal language I was given was itself hopelessly dead and inadequate. Even where it did seem to have wonderful resources, these were, to put it mildly, not always taken full advantage of by lawyers and judges—who sometimes spoke in the dead ways familiar to all of us, full of clichés and empty formulas.

But both things—the inherent failings of the language and our failings in our use of it—seemed to me to present challenges for a life of value, the aim of which was to define and express meaning: the meaning of the experience of our clients; the meaning of the collection of texts and traditions and understandings that are the embodiment of the law; the meaning of the institutions of thought and argument in which these questions were presented and addressed.[2]

When I went into law practice the view I describe was confirmed: the heart of my work was reading and writing, not in a trivial or mechanical sense, not as the exercise of skill alone, but as the fullest and most important expression of a mind engaged in the world. As we have seen with

---

in drafting documents the same was true: the lawyers were always testing what they were writing by imagining a dispute in court.

2. I have been talking of the life of the lawyer as one of speaking and writing, but, as I have urged in the earlier chapters of this book, it was of course one of reading as well. One had to learn how to read texts written in other times and places, on other occasions, by other people, and bring them intelligently and coherently into the present, so that they might speak to the difficulty or dispute we were facing. This kind of reading, like the writing, was a task that could never be performed perfectly. It required imagination, learning, and intelligence, all of the highest order you could achieve. And even with all the talents in the world, the coherence would still be imperfect, the argument flawed, the understanding incomplete—a fact that for me opened up a future full of interest and value.

respect to the Model Penal Code and the opinions of Justice Holmes it was hard to do it well, impossible to do it perfectly.

I saw law, as I continue to see it, as an activity of mind and language, a way of claiming meaning for experience and making that meaning real. It is not merely a system of rules, as I said in chapter one, but a structure of thought and expression that is built upon a set of inherently unstable, dynamic, and dialogic tensions. In this it is like a poem.

Tensions in Legal Thought and Expression

Exactly what are the tensions of which I speak, and how do they work? How are they to be addressed? What does it mean that the law is built upon them? These are my next questions.

I should make clear at the outset that much of what I am going to say may seem very basic. Indeed it *is* basic. At one time perhaps we could have taken much of what I am going to say for granted. This set of perceptions might not have been wholly conscious, but I think it was there in the legal culture, and did not need stating.

Between Legal Language and Ordinary Language

It may help us uncover some of the tensions upon which legal discourse is built if we think of a day in the life of the lawyer I was preparing to become, starting with the moment when the client comes into our office seeking our help.

THE CLIENT'S STORY

This client—whether a person or corporation or government body—will have a story to tell and a language in which to tell it. Perhaps he will tell us about domestic violence that he or his children have suffered; perhaps about an idea that he and two others have for forming a corporation that will create and sell computer software; perhaps about the bank's threat to foreclose the mortgage on his house.

The problem can be mundane and ordinary, or sophisticated and rare, but in any case our client will have his own sense of what is wrong, of what he wants, and of his own incapacity to get it on his own. He will turn to us, after all, only when he sees that he needs help.

His story will be cast in his ordinary language, the way he usually thinks and speaks. Our job is to listen to him talk in his language, and then to ask questions that will prompt him to say more. For our knowledge of the law should enable us to raise issues that he will not have thought of, and in this way to encourage a fuller statement of his story, cast in the language of the law.

When is his story complete? When do we have everything we need to know? A very good question. The sea of possibly relevant facts is infinite, and there is no clear way of knowing when we have enough. In such conversations there is a circular dependence between facts and law: the facts determine what law is relevant, the law determines what facts are relevant.[3] In principle we could go on forever, but we stop when we think we have enough to enable us to develop our case.

No rules could tell us when we have reached this point; our sense of completeness is a judgment we gradually make, as we go back and forth between his story and what we know of the law. It rests upon our educated intuition.

TRANSLATION

Our second task will be to translate what we have been told by our client into legal language. This requires us to go from his or her language to the law and back again, over and over, checking both his story and our translation of it. As with all translations, this process is inherently imperfect and distorting. It cannot be done to a formula or rule, but requires the exercise of an art.

Sometimes the gap between our languages seems on the surface rather small, for example at closing argument, when we are speaking to the jury and doing so in a language as close to ordinary English as we can manage.[4] Sometimes the gap is enormous. When our client hears us make an argument about choice of law—maintaining, for example, that Nebraska law should apply, not Iowa law, or federal law rather than state law—she may not see any connection at all with the problem she brought to us. But the choice of law problem, if it is a real one, is one of the ways the law gives meaning to her case. It may even be that what this

3. I owe this observation to Professor Albert Sacks, who made this illuminating comment in a classroom more than 50 years ago.

4. This appearance can be illusory. Beneath the surface of what seems ordinary English in the lawyer's argument one can often discern important legal judgments and arguments.

case will ultimately stand for in the law is a new and persuasive approach to choice of law, something she may not care about at all.

Our first tension in the law, then, is the one between ordinary and legal language. The lawyer has to speak both languages; he or she has to translate, as well as possible, both ways, into the law and out of it, a process that is at every stage defective or imperfect. Sometimes the defect will be fatal: we will simply not be able to say in the language we are given what we think should be said about this case.[5]

This tension can be found not only in interviews with the client, but throughout the process, and in many forms: in the lawyer's examination or cross-examination of lay witnesses, for example; in her closing argument to the jury, who are of course untrained in the law; and even in her arguments with the opposing counsel and to the judge, for it is common there to resort to ordinary life and language for images with which to make a point. Everyone in the law wants to be able to say in ordinary terms what she is saying in legal terms, and vice versa.

THE INEXPRESSIBLE

This tension is made more difficult by the existence of a related one, between language of any kind at all and the mute world of inexpressible experience. In an important sense the client's story can never fully be told even in ordinary English. There is always a level of experience that cannot be adequately expressed in any language: what a broken arm actually feels like, for example, or the helpless rage and agony of seeing your children hurt by your spouse, or the mute sense of outrage or betrayal at a business partner's disloyalty. Everything we say, in any language, floats as it were on a sea of inexpressible experience.

We face then not only a tension between legal and other forms of language and expression, but a tension between the world of words and the world of mute experience that underlies it.

These tensions are inherently unstable, never fully resolvable. Responding to them is not matter of logic, or ends-means rationality, or conceptual analysis, but rather requires an art, an art of language and judgment.

---

5. In such a case we are effectively silenced. For an example see *The Legal Imagination*, 187–195 (1973, 2018).

Between Law and Other Specialized Languages

The tension between legal and ordinary speech just described is in a sense an instance of a larger tension, our second, arising from the fact that legal discourse is itself built upon many different voices, many different languages. It speaks not with one voice but with many voices, and its meaning to a large degree lies in the music that is made among them.

Thus in our country we have the official voices of the legislature, the trial judge, the Constitution, the Supreme Court, each speaking in its own way to the others, and to the public too—and this not only at the national level, but in each of the fifty states.

We also have witnesses, expert and inexpert, each speaking from his or her point of view in the world. The voice of the person who saw the robbery, of the policeman who investigated it, of the technician who tested the blood, of the robbery victim himself; the voice of the defendant, of the psychiatrist testifying on the question of his sanity, of the witness who claims he saw the victim begin the fracas by attacking the defendant; all these are different voices, speaking in different languages.

Suppose for example that our case is a medical malpractice case, in which each side plans to call two expert witnesses—a heart surgeon, say, and an engineer who knows about mechanical heart valves. To prepare our own witnesses for direct and cross examination, and to cross-examine the opposition witnesses, we shall need to learn something of the languages of the doctor and engineer. We must be prepared to translate, that is, not only between ordinary language and legal language, but between both of these languages and a range of specialized languages.[6] This activity of translation is both necessary and inherently imperfect.

It is sometimes thought that the law is a single language of authority, a set of nested commands, running from the general to the particular, all in the same voice of absolute or legislative authority, but as we see here such a view makes little sense. The lawyer or judge must be an artist in translation, prepared to translate between the world of mute experience

---

6. An obvious difficulty is that we cannot really learn the language of doctor or engineer with the kind of completeness and depth that only those professionals can have. How then do we face this impossible task? Partly, we are schooled by our own witnesses, and by other advisers as well; partly, we read in the field in question in order to learn its language as well as we can; partly, we test, over and over, what the expert says by translating it into ordinary language we can understand. But we never have it perfectly.

and the world of words; between ordinary language and legal language; and between both of these and specialized languages as well.

Perhaps we do not teach translation of this kind in law school but we certainly should.

Between Opposing Lawyers

There is a third tension, very different in kind, that is also fundamental to the legal process: the tension that exists between the lawyers on opposing sides of the case. This tension is plain: we want our client to win, she wants hers to win, and each of us will do all we properly can to make that happen.

COMPETITIVE TENSION

At trial each lawyer will stretch every nerve to present the material of the law, and the facts, in such a way as to fit with the fundamental claims of his or her client. One uses the voice of condemnation or attack, the other of excuse or defense. We are deeply opposed, for each of us is straining to create a sense of the case, and the law, that will lead the judge or jury to decide our way. This is a power struggle in the law, and it creates an inherently unstable tension, one that is by nature both dynamic and dialogic.

Yet, as I suggested in chapter one, there is something odd here: while we and the lawyer on the other side are obviously opposed to each other, we are also in fact cooperating. We agree in a general way, for example, both about the materials relevant to our argument and about the way it should proceed. While we are strenuously disagreeing, that is, we are equally strenuously affirming a great deal: the language, the conventions of discourse, the principles or understandings by which we carry on our argument, many of the authorities we both invoke, and certain conclusions too, on questions both of law and fact.

We contest what we can, but we accept what we cannot, and this becomes, for the moment at least, a firm foundation for further thought on both sides. We thus affirm the constraints of the law within which we find that we, despite our strongest efforts, must operate.

When our joint performance works well—as it of course does not always do—it subjects the material of the law, and the facts too, to a most intense and searching scrutiny. Instead of seeking the single meaning of the statutes, of the judicial opinions, of the regulations, and of other materials of authority, we two lawyers together are demonstrating the range of possible meanings that these texts may reasonably be given, and using all our powers to do this. In our hands, that is, the law is not a closed system of significances, but is systematically opened up to new possibilities — opened up, in fact, as far as we can manage. That is one of the points of our work.

This tension between competing voices and perspectives gives a special kind of life to the law. As I just said, it creates a space for newness and creativity in reading the texts of the law, which might otherwise be read in dead and mechanical ways.

It is also a way of being a grown-up: learning to live in a world in which people think differently from each other and to respect the judgments of those with whom we disagree.

MORAL TENSION

This very process, rhetorical and adversarial in nature, creates a related tension, an internal one, moral or ethical in nature, within each of the lawyers. Is what she is doing justifiable, or even respectable?

We are making arguments for our client, on the law and the facts; but suppose we do not think that what we are arguing for is right? Suppose we think that the other side should win? Or, perhaps more likely, suppose we do not allow ourselves to think at all about the right result, about what justice requires, but only about what arguments will work? What have we become?

This problem can be swept under the rug by claiming that the adversarial system works to produce justice, so that even if we are not arguing justly, the system will be just — if not in this particular case, most of the time. But that claim rests on an unprovable optimism, and in any event does not address the most important ethical issue, which is who we are becoming when we engage in the activity I describe. Are we just mouthpieces who will say anything to win, whether or not we mean it? Or can we see ourselves as doing something we can truly respect?

A book could be written about this issue,[7] but I hope that you can already see that here is another tension, inherently unstable, deep within the lawyer himself or herself. It is unavoidable by a conscientious person.

---

7. For my own efforts at dealing with this problem, see chapter four of *When Words Lose Their Meaning* (1984) and chapter nine of *Heracles' Bow* (1986).

It is not susceptible of systemic resolution, by resort to a slogan or a rule or a phrase, but must be addressed over and over in the life of the lawyer, in the deep particulars of every argument he or she makes.

Between Competing but Plausible Readings of the Law

For our next tension, let us assume that the efforts at negotiation have failed and that the case is headed for court, where the two lawyers will speak to the judge who will decide between them.

If we imagine ourselves for a moment as the judge, we can see that the tension between the lawyers creates, or ought to create, a parallel tension in our own mind, as the two opposing voices are present and alive within us. If we start to think one way, we should find ourselves checked by the other.

COMPETING VERSIONS OF THE LAW

The elaboration by the lawyers of arguments on both sides is, among other things, a way of resisting the judge's impulse to decide too quickly, by encouraging her to keep her mind open until she has heard it all, thought through it all—indeed it helps her to think it through.

The two sets of arguments, in making explicit the range of possible choices open to the judge, make clear also that the judge will have to make her choice and accept responsibility for it—and not push the decision off on a statute or other text that is read in a conclusory or unthinking way.

This argumentative process demonstrates that the image of the law as a set of clear rules cannot survive a moment's scrutiny. Under the pressure provided by the lawyers' arguments, the scope of judicial choice becomes wide, much wider than one would at first expect. This fact creates a tension right at the heart of the judicial judgment, a tension between rational but opposed conclusions. This is our fourth tension.

If a statute or regulation says that "trucks" must always travel in the right lane, or that imported "toys" pay only half the usual customs duty, or that an arrest may only be made upon "probable cause to believe the suspect has committed a felony" we have a general idea of what is meant to happen, but we also know that elaborate arguments can go on about the meaning of the words, *truck*, *toy*, *probable cause*, *felony*, and even *commit* (does it include aiding and abetting another, or being an accessory after the fact?). Legal categories, whether legislative or judicial in origin, thus invariably carry a substantial range of reasonable possibilities for their meaning, sometimes a very wide range. Among these possibilities the judge will have to choose. How is she to do this?

A great deal has been written on this question, with answers ranging at least across the following spectrum: (1) the uncertainty of meaning creates in her a discretionary power to do whatever she wants; (2) she is to be guided in the exercise of her discretion by her sense of the intention of the rule-maker; (3) she is to be guided by appropriate general principles of moral and political philosophy; (4) she is to be guided by natural law; (5) she is to be guided by analogy to other legal examples; (6) she is to resolve the ambiguity against the drafter of the document, since he or she is responsible for it; and so on.

I will not join in the debate as to which of these, or others, should guide her decision. It is enough for present purposes that it is clear that in her basic task of legal decision-making the judge inhabits a zone marked by a strong tension between alternative ways of thinking, a tension that is, like the other ones I have described, dynamic, dialogic, and inherently unstable. The resolution of this tension, like the other ones, cannot be achieved simply by reference to a rule or practice or phrase or idea, but must be achieved afresh, in every case, by an art of judgment. This very fact gives life to the law.

TENSIONS WITHIN THE JUDGE

As the judge faces this problem, she also faces her own version of what I earlier called the tension between the world of language and the world of inexpressible experience. This tension arises within her the moment she asks herself how and why the case should be decided.

Here is what I mean. A part of her mind will think in terms of legal arguments of the kind we have been discussing, testing them against each other for their force and power. Sometimes this will lead her to a decision about which she feels confident and comfortable, both when she makes it and afterwards. She will feel that there is no need to examine further what she did or why.

But sometimes she will be aware that beneath that layer of the mind is another, an intuitive center—educated by experience and reflection, disciplined by the arguments she has heard and her own commitment to neutrality—that is seeking the right decision in a case she recognizes as hard. In these cases, the judge knows that her written opinion can never express or justify what the center of herself is doing, the secret spring of judgment at her core. Her opinion therefore, however honestly written, can have some of the characteristics of a false pretense: "This is why I decided the case as I did," the opinion says; but the judge knows that the true springs of decision are deep within her, and can never be fully known or explained. The tension this creates cannot be resolved in any a priori way by a rule or principle, but must, like the others mentioned, be lived through in detail and addressed anew every time it arises. And in retrospect it may arise more often than she was aware of at the time.

Between Substance and Procedure

A fifth structural tension runs through the law: between what we call "substance," on the one hand, and procedural or institutional considerations on the other.

One of the deepest—and to the lay person, most mystifying—characteristics of legal thought is that the lawyers and judges seem to think about both kinds of questions at once, working as it were in two channels simultaneously. Whenever the lawyers argue about a substantive question, such as the meaning of a statutory or constitutional provision, they are likely at the same time to argue about a procedural question: the requirements for a judgment on the pleadings, for example, or for summary judgment, or for a directed verdict.

This second channel, which I am calling "procedural," is by no means limited to technical matters of judicial procedure, but includes arguments of a much more general kind, which might be called "institutional."

Suppose the substantive question is whether a certain company may dump industrial wastewater in the river; or whether a school on an Indian reservation may begin its days with the recitation of a sentence that sums up the traditional wisdom of the tribe; or whether one may have a loud party to celebrate a child's graduation from school, even though the neighbors object.

The lawyer or judge facing such substantive questions will at the same time face a set of institutional questions: Who is empowered to decide this question in the first instance, and why? What procedures should this actor be compelled to follow, and why? To what review is the first actor's judgment to be subjected, and why? Or, to reverse the point of view, to what degree of deference is it to be entitled, and why?

Suppose for example in the water discharge case that there is a municipal ordinance on the subject. Here the lawyers will ask what I have been calling the substantive question—whether the ordinance should be interpreted to prohibit this discharge—but at the same time a set of institutional questions: whether the city council was authorized to pass such an ordinance by the relevant statute; if so, whether it followed the requisite procedures; if so, whether this ordinance, even if authorized by statute, meets the requirements of the state or federal constitution. In fact much of what we mean by constitutional law is institutional in just this way, determining what agency should have the power to decide what questions, under what procedures, and subject to what review.

The mind of the lawyer or judge mysteriously works in both tracks at once, and there is an inherently unstable tension between them. Sometimes, indeed, the two lines of thought intertwine in such a way as to make them one. We just cannot think of one without the other. What happens in one line of thought affects the other. It is like seeing that the smooth and rough sides of a piece of cloth each require and imply the other.

There is no way to draft a set of rules for resolving this tension. Like the others, it must be addressed by an art of language and judgment.

Between the Particular and the General

Whenever a judge decides a case, especially when he explains his decision, there is another way in which he is functioning on two different levels at once, with a strong tension between them. At one level are the parties to this particular case, and what justice between them seems to require; at another level is thought about the whole class of cases in some way like this, with similar issues, similar problems. The judge's job is to do justice at both levels; something similar is true of the attorneys on both sides, each of whom must try to maintain that justice of both kinds, not just one, requires a favorable outcome for him or her.

To take a common example: a man under pressure from his creditors files a fraudulent income tax return, one that hides much of his income and claims deductions to which he is not entitled. He is convicted of tax fraud and the moment for sentencing arrives: is the judge to shape the sentence to the individual person or to the whole class of offenders to which this person belongs? The judge knows he is very unlikely to commit this offense again, in part because the IRS will keep an eye on him and in part because the whole experience of trial has been utterly mortifying to him. (Let us also suppose that his financial distress has been greatly eased by an inheritance.)

His lawyer will say no purpose is served by sending this man to prison. He should be put on probation.

The prosecutor will say that the judge's job is not just to do justice in this case, but to advance the cause of justice in cases like it. To give this man probation will greatly reduce the force of the signal sent by his conviction. Other potential violators will hope that they too will receive leniency, because their cases will be equally sympathetic. The conviction will not deter others as it is properly meant to do.

What is the judge to do?

This tension is in fact built into the form of legal rules, the basic way in which law is made by legislators and courts alike. The rule is cast in general categories, which are in the nature of things what lawyers call underinclusive and overinclusive—that is, they include what they are not really meant to include, and they fail to reach all the cases they are meant to reach. Take something as simple as speed limits, say a limit of 70 mph on a highway. The idea of the rule is to make us safe from each other (and ourselves), but we know that there are drivers who keep within the limit who are not safe, yet cannot usually be ticketed. There may also be drivers who can safely exceed that limit, especially on a clear highway with little traffic, but they can be ticketed, and cannot claim in defense that they were in fact driving as safely as people who stay within the limit.

Throughout the law one must face a tension between the general categories in which rules are properly drawn and the circumstances of particular cases, a tension that must be freshly addressed every time it can be seen.

Between Law and Justice

A seventh tension, still different from the others, exists at the heart of legal thought, between the twin demands of law and justice. For in our system the lawyer and judge alike must ask not only, "What does the law require?" but "What does justice require?"

As I said in chapter one, it is a convention of our law—I have never seen it plainly stated but seems to me undeniable—that in every case the lawyer on each side must maintain that the result he or she is arguing for is both required by the law and itself fundamentally just. An argument that claimed that the law required the outcome, but admitted that the result was unjust, would be profoundly incomplete. No lawyer would want to be in the position of making such a case. Likewise incomplete would be the sister argument which claimed that justice required the result that is argued for, but admitted that the law was against it. Nor would a judge happily admit in her opinion either that her judgment was unjust or that it was against the law.[8]

In this sense ours is a system of both natural and positive law. It is like a chariot being drawn by two horses: they often pull in opposed directions, but unruly and uncooperative as they may be, together they take the chariot in a direction that is much better than that towards which either of the horses alone is pulling it.

The immense and deep tension between these two claims means that the lawyer or judge must often labor to harmonize them, sometimes to the breaking point. But it also gives both lawyer and judge an opportunity to create something new and alive: not merely the logical working out of rules or premises, but a deep engagement both with the texts of the past and the facts of the present, and what they mean. It is one aspect of the lawyer's great task, which is to bring into one field of vision the ideal and the real.[9]

---

8. Sometimes a judge may feel compelled to decide a case in a way he thinks unjust simply because the statute or contract or regulation at issue cannot in his view bear another reading. In these situations the judge is issuing an order or decision he thinks unjust, but it is not he who is responsible for this fact. One difficult question for him is whether, and how, he should express his own judgment that the result he is compelled to reach is unjust. Maybe he should, but if so I think he should also express the reasons why he thinks it right—indeed just—that he should follow the statutory or other rules that he thinks unjust.

9. Consider, for example, the fact that we talk to the judge not as the bundle of prejudices and beliefs and commitments and character traits that form part of his or her character, but as an ideal judge, one who is always seeking to do justice under the law. Likewise, we idealize the legislature, interpreting its words as if they came from a wise and good person, when of course the truth is more complex. We idealize our client too in the way we talk about her, presenting her in the best light possible. In this sense we are engaged in work that is explicitly aspirational in character.

At the same time we are required to be realists, about all these actors and about the process too, recognizing that the legislature is a political body, that the judge is biased for us or against us, that our client has all the usual faults of humanity: she may lie to us, or not pay the fine or our bill; she may skip town.

Between the Past and Present — and the Future Too

Finally let me suggest one more tension, a temporal one: between the past and the present, and between both of them and the future.[10]

The task of the lawyer and judge is to bring the materials of the past — sometimes recent past, sometimes remote past — to bear on the problems of the present, and in so doing to make something new for the future. The law is thus not a static or timeless system, working out the implications of its premises in abstract or purely logical ways, but a way of functioning in a world dominated by time, seizing the ever-passing moment of the present as the place to join past and future. It is a way of defining experience; learning from experience; shaping experience.

This tension is present in all legal argument, but most of all in the special form we call the judicial opinion. This text brings together all that the parties have been able to invoke from the past, and issues the authoritative judgment that speaks to the future. It does not just state or define a rule, but issues a judgment, which it explains, and explains in ways that go beyond the language of the rule itself.

Addressing These Tensions in Writing

I am saying, then, that legal thought is at its heart not a top-down elaboration of the meaning of a set of rules by a process of logic or end-means rationality; nor is it a pattern of conduct that can be adequately represented and understood in the language of social science; rather, it is an activity of mind and language, one that is deeply marked by a set of structural tensions, or clusters of tensions:

- between ordinary language and legal language (indeed between language itself, of any kind, and the mute world that lies beneath it);

10. Another tension one could add to the list is the tension in the mind of the lawyer or judge between narrative and theory, for these modes of thought work in very different ways. See *The Legal Imagination,* 858–926, 624–86 (1973, 2018). One might also think about the tensions that the legislator must face as he or she gives shape to a statute, discussed *id.* 195–242.

- between a multiplicity of voices, speaking from different positions within the legal order, or outside of it, in a variety of specialized and expert languages;
- between opposed lawyers, each of whom seems to resist the other at every point, though in another way they are cooperating deeply;
- within each lawyer, whenever she asks what it means for herself and the world that she is acting as she is;
- between many conflicting but justifiable ways of giving meaning to the rules and principles of law, among which the judge will have to choose;
- between the reasoning and intuitive capacities of the judge herself;
- between substantive and procedural (or institutional) lines of thought, a tension that runs throughout the law;
- between the general and the particular;
- between the imperatives of law and justice;
- between the past and the present, the present and the future, for law lives in time and out of shared experience.

This is not an exhaustive list, but for present purposes it will do.

Each of these tensions is, as I have said, inherently unstable, that is, not resolvable by reference to fixed rules, principles, or conventions; each is dynamic, not static, thus moving us in new directions that we cannot always anticipate; each is dialogic, acting with the force of competing voices at work in the world or in the self. These tensions interact, to create fault lines that run through every act of full legal analysis. Their management is essential to the work of lawyer or judge.

Consequences

What happens if we start to think of law in this way?

The Law Is Not the Rules

Let me suggest, to start with, that it makes simply impossible the view that the law is just a system or scheme of rules that are in practice applied more or less rationally to produce a set of intended or desired results.

This is a view that law students often bring to law school with them. They expect that we shall teach them a set of rules. These are the rules they will apply as lawyers, and knowledge of them is what sets them apart from the nonlawyer, to whom they are unknown. A large part of a good legal education is disabusing them of this view.

There are many reasons that such an image is attractive to the student. It explains the kind of knowledge that the lawyer has, and justifies her role (and her fees). It is also in principle simple, even easy: if all I have to do is memorize a set of rules, even if there are a lot of them, I am confident that I can do it. The work may be dull but it won't be hard. It won't ask of me what I cannot already do; it will not ask me to change and grow. So it is natural for the student to say: "I want the law to be a set of rules!"[11]

But I think a view of law as rules is also at work in the kind of scholarship and teaching that takes as its subject the question, not how lawyers think and should think, but what the rules should be. We see this view at work in policy studies generally, in "law and economics" in particular, in much jurisprudence, and indeed wherever the tendency to abstract or theoretical thinking has taken hold, whether in the analysis of legislative or judicial problems.

The Law Is Not Policy

The question of social policy is of course an important one, and lawyers, economists, social scientists, moral philosophers, ordinary people, and lots of others too, can properly speak to it.

But it is not the essential question for either lawyer or judge, who is instead repeatedly asked to deal with the particulars of a case, whether as adviser, advocate, or decider, and to do so in light of the whole structure of arguably relevant and authoritative legal rules, principles, conventions, precedents, understandings, indeed in light of the whole legal world and culture. This structure, as I have been trying to show, is not a coherent conceptual system but a dramatic and rhetorical process

11. It was once common for law teachers to think that one of the structural tensions in the classroom was over this issue, and we typically insisted, against resistance, that we were teaching something other than rules, namely how lawyers think, and think well. In teaching criminal law, for example, I handed out the first day a page which had on it all the rules we would learn that term. I told the students that they could memorize them in an hour at most. What this meant was that whatever the rest of the course was about, it was not learning the rules.

marked by a series of deep tensions that cannot be reduced to or governed by a system of rules or other directives.[12]

Rules of the standard legislative (or judicial) form do exist, and they serve to guide general expectations and behavior. They are important and can be of course talked about in such terms. But this is not the level at which the judge or lawyer works, for these people are normally called upon only when there is a problem or difficulty, a moment at which the rules collide with reality, or each other, and do not work in the easy way they are thought to do. To put it in a phrase, the judge and lawyer deal not with the "rules" as such, as a discrete conceptual system, but with what happens when that abstract language, and the rest of the authoritative language of the law, meets the world.

The Law Establishes a Set of Possibilities for Original Thought and Expression

The law is not a system, but a way of managing the relations between what looks like a system and many dimensions of actual life: the experience of the client and lawyer, including the experience that cannot be expressed in any language at all; the multiplicity of languages and voices that make up our world; the conflicts and harmonies between opposing lawyers; the freedom and responsibility of the judge; the idealistic and realistic tendencies of legal thought; the tension between past and present, present and future.

The way in which lawyer and judge think about the moment at which the language of the law meets the world is to engage in a complex process of thought that is built upon and marked by tensions of the sort I have summarized.[13] As I have said, these cannot be resolved by reference to any set of directives or guides, but must be addressed afresh whenever

12. For a similar argument from a different point of view see A. W. Brian Simpson, "The Common Law and Legal Theory," in *Oxford Essays on Jurisprudence, Second Series* 79 (1973).

13. This is true of the teacher as well, of course. When I think of my own decision to teach law rather than practice it, and of the claim, by some, that this was a retreat to the Ivory Tower from the Real World, I want to say that teaching, properly done, is itself a form of practice, a way of facing the set of tensions I describe here. To do this one must regard the cases not simply as instances of theoretical questions or the application of rules, but as pieces of the whole process of legal argument and thought, as I have sketched it here, from the interview with the client to the appeal of an adverse judgment.

the lawyer or judge goes to work, and always in light of the particulars of the case in which they are presented. The lawyer and judge do not operate simply at the level of high generality that the rules mark out, nor simply at the level of particularity established by the facts of the case, but always in an uneasy tension between these two levels of thought. They are in this like poets, who also face the tension between particular and general in all that they do.[14]

In saying all this, let me stress, I am trying to define what I see to be the positive possibilities of life in the law. Of course these possibilities are not attained automatically, and never fully or perfectly, and sometimes they are corrupted. Often enough lawyers or judges are thoughtless, crude, unimaginative, inarticulate, and dull. Indeed such things are sometimes true of us all. But not always, in every way. My effort here is to offer an image of the activity of law at its most demanding and fulfilling, by which we can shape our efforts as we practice or teach it—an image, over the horizon, as it were, which we can keep before us as we do our work, a sense of how things might be if only we could make them so.

The law does not work its way to predetermined conclusions through a process of iron logic, but almost the opposite: it is a set of possibilities for original thought and expression. It is not a totalitarian system, closed and unlistening, but an open system, like a language, not only making creativity possible, but requiring it. The process in which we are engaged is an art of testing and invention.

Every case, every legal conversation, is an opportunity to exercise the lawyer's complex art of mind and imagination, the art it is one purpose of this book to define. This art is what we teach, what we practice, and what we cherish.[15]

---

14. Sir Philip Sidney said that philosophy deals with mere abstractions, history with mere particulars; the poet alone "doth perform both." *The Defense of Poesie* (1595). (For an accessible copy of the text see Roy Lamson and Hallett Smith, *The Golden Hind: An Anthology of Elizabethan Prose and Poetry, 280* (rev.ed. 1956).

15. The voice that says, "I have a theory that answers this and all such questions," is not the voice of lawyer or judge. If they are to do their jobs well those actors must speak in much more complex, tentative, exploratory ways, sensitive, like the poet, to the constant tensions between various lines of thought and meaning.

The Law Is an Art of Mind and Language

In calling what the lawyer and judge engage in an *art*, I have in mind the thought that all art—whether music or painting or architecture or poetry or drama—proceeds by way of tension and resolution: a conflict is stated or hinted at or felt; the tension between opposing elements is developed and expanded; and at the end a resolution is reached—but never a final resolution, only a momentary one. When one poem or sonata is finished, another is to be begun, and so it is with legal argument and legal judgment. The aim of the lawyer, as for the poet, to quote Robert Frost, is to end "in a clarification of life—not necessarily a great clarification, such as sects and cults are founded on, but in a momentary stay against confusion."[16]

The tensions I have been defining are not, then, as some might say, simply "noise in the system," but the life of the law itself.[17]

This vision of the law is in a sense an old-fashioned one, going back to the roots of legal thought in the West, in the study and practice of the art of rhetoric. At its heart it is a vision of law as an art of language and judgment, an art of the maintenance and repair of human culture and community.[18] In another sense, however, it is not old-fashioned at all, but as timely as it ever was. In my view it is necessary to have such a vision if, in our practice and teaching and judging, the law is to fulfill its nature and its promise.

---

16. Robert Frost, "The Figure a Poem Makes," in *Robert Frost: Collected Poems, Prose & Plays*, 776–77 (Poirier and Richardson, eds. 1995).

17. If I am right, what I am saying here has real consequences: for the sort of education that we offer, which should invite the student to engage in the art I describe, not to learn law as a set of rules; for the ethical and intellectual possibilities of the lawyer's life, which can be seen to be far more interesting, challenging, and ethically alive, than the view of the lawyer as rule-applier; and for the expectations that judges can bring to their work and for the ways in which we can evaluate what they do—not simply by political agreement or disagreement with the outcome, but by judging their work as performances of an art, the art of reconciling the ideal and the real.

18. In law, as in poetry, the life and quality of one's work inhere in the way in which constraints are faced, tensions addressed and elaborated, complexities recognized. These things must be done every time afresh. Think of the way a poem is built: it is a structure of meaning in which many forms of expression, each one built on tensions of its own—image, story, meter, rhyme, sentence shape, and so on—interact to create a living whole. There is dynamic tension between or among each of these dimensions, and within them as well, for each presents and responds to a tension between order and disorder. Legal work should be like that.

I have been resisting an image of law as rules and policy, but behind those things is a deeper vision to resist: of law as abstract, mechanical, impersonal, essentially bureaucratic in nature, narrowing rather than broadening the human capacity for experience, understanding, and empathy. To focus on the law as a system, and not on what happens when that system meets the world—and the people of the world—is to strip it of its difficulty, its life, its meaning, and its value.

For it is at this moment, when the law meets the world—in the work of lawyer, judge, or teacher—that it can become most fully alive. This moment contains within it the seeds of resistance to the forces of mindless empire and control, for every case is an opportunity for newness of thought, for creativity and surprise, for the introduction into the world of power an unrecognized voice, language, or claim.

In the moment of speech, or writing, there is always the possibility that one can bring the world into new life.

What Does This Mean about Justice?

So far in this chapter I have talked mainly about law. I want now to say something about what this view of law means for our understanding of justice and for the ways we try to make justice real in the world.

First let me suggest that while we can think and talk about justice in many ways, two in particular stand out for lawyers: as an abstract matter, as philosophers typically do, or as an institutional matter, as lawyers typically do.

We talk about justice *abstractly* when we think about what the world should be like as though we could make it whatever we wanted, writing on a clean slate. Thus we might say that in a just country there would be universal education and health care, no death penalty for crimes, public support for the arts, and women's control over their bodies. These are not self-evident truths, however, and someone might say in response that in a just country education and health care and the arts would all be governed by the market, which is the most efficient and hence just allocator of human goods, that the death penalty would be used in cases of murder, and that women's control of their bodies would never include the killing of a human fetus.

These are familiar positions, both ways, and as a matter of social fact, highly arguable. When we talk in an abstract way about which of these positions, or what combination of them, is just or unjust, we are free to use every resource at our disposal, from self-evidence, to social theory, to religious truth, to public opinion. But we have to recognize that, whatever we believe, others might come to an opposite conclusion. There is no arbiter, no one who can tell us that this is truly just, that truly unjust. We are debating competing conceptions of social justice.

When we talk about justice as an *institutional* matter, by contrast, we are by definition no longer writing on a clean slate. We recognize that power and authority are already distributed among many actors, present and past, each of whom has his or her own zone of authority. If made within their jurisdiction, their judgments are entitled to some degree of respect even if we disagree with them—the precise degree of respect being an important question both of law and justice. In talking about what is just or unjust for a particular actor to do in this larger context, no one can simply claim that justice should be whatever seems right to him or her, without regard to what others think and say. Others have spoken, or will speak, with some degree of authority, and respect must be given to their judgments.

Thus what is seen as a single question in the conversation about abstract justice—e.g., is the death penalty unjust?—in an institutional context becomes many questions. For example we could ask: How, if at all, does the Constitution speak to the death penalty, either in the eighth amendment (prohibiting cruel and unusual punishment), in the due process or equal protection clauses, or elsewhere? Even to think about this question requires one to read, understand, and judge not only the text of the Constitution but many cases decided under it, both by state and federal judges. We should also ask: is there a federal statute that could be read to speak to the issue, or a provision of state law, whether legislative, judicial, or constitutional? How are these texts to be read, alone and with each other? Each of these actors may have spoken to the matter and it is a real and vital question, a question indeed of justice, how far each judgment is to be respected, and why.

In evaluating what official speakers have to say, we will want to turn to certain unofficial speakers as well: sociologists who have studied how the death penalty works, perhaps with special attention to racial discrimination; psychologists who can talk about the experience of execution, for the executed and executors alike; philosophers who explain why or why not such execution violates the Kantian categorical imperative; literary critics, who can explicate the ways in which language, and law, can respect the fundamental humanity of people or dehumanize them; and so on.

As I said earlier, one of the tensions in the law is that between its own form of discourse and others. One judgment we would need to make in deciding how just the law was would focus on exactly that relationship: Were the legal speakers unduly deferential to (or unduly dismissive of) nonlegal sources of authority? All of these investigations take place in the context I have described above, namely a legal system defined by its tensions—tensions that must be addressed and thought about, not simply swept away. To work well with the tensions I describe is itself to achieve an important kind of justice; this kind of justice is no less important than abstract justice; indeed if abstract justice is to become real, and not merely abstract, it must itself be wisely, justly, and artfully located in the context of these tensions. It is not too much to say that in this process lies the only hope for justice in the law.

In this chapter I have traced out a series of tensions that seem to me inescapably present to one working with law in our tradition. To pretend they are not there is I think a kind of cop-out; to face them, knowing that you cannot completely resolve them, is daunting, to say the least. How can we best equip ourselves for the task?

It may help to recognize that it is not only people of the law who face tensions in their work. Think of the historian, who must constantly negotiate the tension between the presentation of facts and the meanings he or she wants to claim for them. The psychologist must face a similar tension between the generalizations learned in graduate school and the rich particular detail offered by his or her client. The economist must face the tension between the logical rationality of his or her theory and complex mysteries of actual economic life. As I suggest above, virtually all forms of art depend upon the creation or recognition of a tension, which is partly, but only partly, resolved.

In these instances, and others from other fields, how do you suppose such tensions can be addressed, well and badly? What kind of resolution is possible? It might be worthwhile to write out a couple of pages in which you address one of the problems that was central to your undergraduate major, in the language and method of that major. What tensions are present here and how to you address them? How is what you are doing here like or unlike law as we have been defining it?

Or to bring the question home to law: what would it be like to try to write a treatise on constitutional law that recognized and addressed the tensions I have described?

Now a question about our legal culture: If you are a lawyer, or otherwise a reader of law, do you think that the tensions I describe above are in fact alive and recognized in what you read? Or is legal discourse losing some of its life and meaning? If so, how and why? If so, what can be done about it?

5

Law, Economics, and Torture

Until now my object has been to define, by extended examples, the workings of legal thought and judgment of a kind that I admire, and which I think have done much to create our culture and to hold together our public world. This has been meant as a partial definition of the kind of law—and the democracy it both depends on and maintains—that I think we should work to keep alive. As I hope has been clear, I have invited you to participate in this branch of our culture by responding to what you read and by thinking about those responses.

I said in the Foreword that this kind of law is under serious threat in our world, and in this chapter I offer an introduction to some of the cultural forces that are working against the law as I have been defining it.

Here I consider a set of deeply related themes: the fact that we have allowed economic inequality in our country to increase to obviously indefensible levels; what that inequality means for the life and structure of our democratic republic; the transformation or erosion of law, in the sense in which I have been presenting it, even in law schools and the law courts; the pressure for lawyers and policymakers alike to think in economic terms, a kind of thinking that tends to destroy legal thought; the fact that torture was practiced and publicly defended in our country for several years, and may be again; the way torture has been justified, mainly by a kind of cost-benefit analysis, which works as an acid that destroys everything but itself; the appearance of other forms of deliberate dehumanization by our govern-

ment; and the loss of the sense that the search for justice is at the heart of our common life.[1]

As you will see, the conditions I describe bring our country close to the position taken by the Athenians in the famous Melian dialogue, which is that justice is a topic of argument only between equals; when one side has the power it does what it wants, and the weak must comply or die. Then justice dies.

In these circumstances it is hard to imagine how law can be kept alive. That will be the topic of my last chapter.

I began this chapter about ten years ago, and two of its main concerns—the evil of economic inequality and the sense of threat to our institutions of law and governance—have become even more salient and threatening, while the third, torture, may seem, as I write this, to recede from public view, but its proponents are powerful once more.

In recent years threats to law and democracy have dramatically increased. In this chapter I make occasional reference to that fact, but I have not tried to update it comprehensively. Things are happening so fast, and so deeply, that this effort would itself be likely to fail. For what it is worth, I mean every word of it as it stands.

As you read it, ask what it means, to you and the world, that we are threatened with the loss of law as we have been defining it. What is at stake here?

IN THE INVITATION TO THE CONFERENCE at which an earlier version of this chapter was presented, the question for each speaker was this: "What most needs to be said about law and democracy under the conditions in which we find ourselves?" The idea was that each of us should address that question in whatever way seemed right to us, as whole minds and complete people, not as experts of some kind. This was an invitation to speak from the center. We wanted to hear what people really thought in the terms in which they thought it.

1. An earlier version of this chapter was originally read at a conference on "Law, Democracy, and the Empire of Force" in 2008. The idea of the conference was to bring together people who would express as directly as they could their respective understandings of the state of American legal and democratic culture, which seemed to all of us to be in a kind of peril we had not known before. The results appear in *Law and Democracy in the Empire of Force* (White and Powell, eds., 2009).

In this chapter I accordingly talk a little differently from the way I usually do. Much of what I say is necessarily impressionistic and personal, and of course I do not ask the reader to accept any of it on my say-so.

Let me urge you to take my reflections rather as a question, which is how far your own experience, your own thinking, is like or unlike my own. Perhaps that way we may be able to illuminate something that is very difficult to think about, namely, significant transformations in the very culture in which we are living. Transformations of this kind have power over our own minds—they do much to form our expectations and to shape what we can say—and the more conscious we can be of them, the better.

As I think about the way things are changing under our feet, a series of phenomena come to my mind. Maybe they are connected, maybe not. That is one of my questions.

Making the Rich Richer

The first of these phenomena is the response—or more properly nonresponse—of the public and the media to the astonishing transfer of national wealth to the very rich that has taken place in our lives. I grew up under Eisenhower, when there was a 90% tax on incomes over $100,000 (roughly a million dollars in our terms), and a general sense that our country was committed to fundamental equality.

This was in part the result of World War II, of which people at every economic level bore the cost, even unto death. It was clear to almost everyone that we were somehow all in this together. The sense of solidarity I mean was expressed in Truman's desegregation of the military and in his proposed civil rights bill, and I think it underlies *Brown v. Board of Education* as well.

The transfer of wealth to a class of superrich began modestly under Kennedy and has taken off in the new millennium. It has clearly been an affirmative goal of the administration that is in power as I write—look at its huge tax break for the rich and very rich—but its roots are much deeper in our world than that. What concerns me here is that in recent years there has been little real thought about this transfer of wealth, certainly not the mass outrage one might have expected. I include law school faculties and students among those unconcerned.

The Consumer Dream and the Ideology of the Market

My question is this: Why has this transfer not been instantly and unanimously resisted by the enormous majority of people at whose expense the rich are multiplying their wealth—most of whom are not doing well economically, some of whom are doing very badly?[2]

This is a matter of mass psychology, and of course I am no expert, but I think the reason is a feeling of helplessness in the face of overwhelming force. I think that the concentration of wealth is not in the eyes of most people a good thing; they feel rather that nothing can be done about it, and that, in a world like this, one had better simply look to his or her own welfare, not large questions of law and democracy.

The rules of the game have somehow shifted over the past twenty years or so; though some people still argue for these things, it seems that we are not really to expect equality, or fairness, or compassion, from our society or its government; we are not to expect decent social and medical services, or clean air, or a mature response to the immense problems of global warming; we are not to expect lawyers and judges to talk in an earnest and serious way about what justice requires. These things are not going to happen, so don't waste your energy complaining. It is a kind of learned helplessness.

Obviously I cannot wholly explain this shift, but one factor seems to me to lie in the way we have come to talk about the nature and purpose of our country, and of human life itself, which is largely in economic terms. For the society as a whole the dominant motive is assumed to be the powerful but empty desire for wealth, without regard to what good or evil that wealth might do; for the individual, felicity is defined largely in terms of ownership and consumption, or, more generally, simple gratification of desire. The "American Dream" is no longer a dream of escape from totalitarian rule and lawless government, as it once was, but a dream of expansive, seemingly unlimited, getting what you want. Of course this way of talking has no place for democratic government—for that requires action, judgment, participation, not mere consumption.

---

2. It is true some of the poor have increased their economic standing, at least a little, over the past decades. But this does not affect my point, for they would have done much better had the wealth we created been more fairly divided. And we ought not kid ourselves about the desperate plight of millions of people in our country. See Kathryn Edin and Luke Shaefer, *$2 a Day: Living on Almost Nothing in America* (2018).

This way of imagining life is not only an empty and trivializing image of human experience,[3] it hides the crucial truth that what the consuming economy in fact creates is not just more opportunity for consumption but power, power in the form of wealth. And great wealth gives great power. As the government withdraws from the regulation of the economy, which it has been doing for decades now, its place is taken by private individuals or private organizations which have immense power over the lives of all of us. This has become much more obvious in the last decade, with a proliferation of politically active billionaires.

The rhetoric supporting this movement often speaks of government as the enemy, and the market as freedom for us all. But the power that is created by the disparity of wealth is real power and, unlike governmental power, it is not shaped or guided by law and democracy. The owners and managers are not elected by the people, not subject to the Constitution, not supposed—or sometimes even allowed—to be motivated by any ideal other than the acquisition of wealth and power.[4]

This arrangement is implicitly—and sometimes explicitly—defended by the argument that this power actually is subject to the control of the people, not through government, but through what is called the discipline of the market, which, the argument runs, is both more efficient and fairer than regulation through law.

But the market cannot be a substitute for democratic government: it has no place or role for any of the institutions through which government works, or for the kind of public deliberation, thought, and argument by which those institutions live; it works not by the principle of one person one vote, but the very different principle of one dollar one vote; and it simultaneously generates and obscures immense imbalances in wealth and power.

The market contains no check on the drive to unlimited economic expansion, a drive that is proving to be suicidal, threatening the living planet upon which everything we are and do depends. It has no place for the concerns of justice as opposed to efficiency, concerns that lie at the heart of democracy.

Those who argue for "getting the government off our backs" are re-

3. See Avner Offer, *The Challenge of Affluence* (2006).

4. For discussion of a debate on this topic at the American Law Institute on corporate purposes, see *From Expectation to Experience*, 111 (1999).

ally arguing for the transfer of power from a democratically responsible government to a regime without any democratic legitimacy at all, indeed without any governing rationality. This is a regime with no place for justice in its thinking or its values, and without the ideal of justice there can be no law.

The consumer dream of our culture teaches us that we have no responsibility for public action, no right to demand meaning in our work and lives, and no obligation for the welfare of others. It induces the sense of learned helplessness I referred to earlier—which is exactly the opposite of the kind of vigorous independence and competence upon which democracy depends.

Advertising and Propaganda

One particularly strong feature of the culture of consumption is an immense and relentless campaign, so pervasive and so normalized as to have become invisible, to persuade the public to accept and act on its premises. I refer here to the world of consumer advertising, especially to its apotheosis in television and on the internet. This kind of advertising persuades people not only to buy this or that item, but more importantly, to accept and live by the whole infantile dream of the consumer economy. It is only in a narrow sense that advertisements compete with each other; in a deeper way they reinforce one another constantly.[5]

Even more disturbingly, this kind of advertising has a direct analogue in the way in which national politics proceeds, for it has become accepted that a political campaign is run like an advertising campaign—though a better word for this cultural form, given its connection with state power, would be propaganda. The political use of propaganda, with the dishonesty that implies, is in now an undeniable part of our life.

Both propaganda and advertising are based on the desire to manipulate others through the use of slogans and clichés and images, sound bites and buzzwords. As they become widespread—active and present in our minds and speech—both forms of speech tend to destroy in us

5. It is worse even than that. As I was preparing an earlier version of this chapter I saw references in the newspaper to the fact, if it is a fact, that virtually all the ads in the broadcast of the then-recent Superbowl contained violence against human beings; and to connect this theme with my next, the torture of human beings, I was told that the number of incidents of torture on mainline TV programs had escalated enormously since our government, under the second President Bush, began its campaign to legalize torture.

the capacity for independent thought and expression upon which self-government depends.

One characteristic of both forms is that nothing is meant, everything is said for the moment, all on the assumption that the people who make up the audience have no memory and no capacity for critical thought. A world is created where thought is not possible.[6] In neither domain — the consumer economy or the world of politics and government — are we defined as responsible participants in a world of shared life and action. Rather, we are manipulated objects, spoken to dishonestly.

The Fact of Empire

So here is my rather glum conclusion. My intuition is that the reason we do not rebel at the immense and unfair transfer of wealth, and all that is associated with it — from golden parachutes for failed CEOs to 60 million dollar bonuses for successful investment bankers to the enormous 2017 tax cut for the very rich — is that in some sense we do not believe that we really have democracy at all any more, at least in the sense in which we once thought we did.[7] Democracy and its law are based on a vision of fundamental equality among human beings, and neither can

6. Here I think of the second President Bush's to me astonishing remark when he was challenged about Guantanamo on a trip to Europe. He said, "I would like to close the camp and put the prisoners on trial" — as though there were some other person, say the President of the United States, who had created Guantanamo in the first place and was now keeping him from closing it. (See *New York Times*, May 8, 2006, page A17.)

A similar effect is achieved by the arguments of government lawyers that such practices as the repeated suffocation known as "waterboarding," electrical shocks, deafening noise, sleep deprivation, threatened attack with dogs on naked prisoners, and so on are not "torture," but only "cruel, inhuman, and degrading," which enables them to say, with all apparent sincerity, and as if we could possibly believe such a thing, that they are opposed to torture too. By such remarks we are invited to join a world where thought is simply not possible — where in Thucydides' terms, "words have lost their meaning." (For more on Thucydides, see chapter three of *When Words Lose Their Meaning* [1984].)

The relevance of this for our day is plain enough. No one can think or talk sensibly in a language of falsehood.

7. I think here of the response of the public and the media to the 2000 election and the Supreme Court case *Bush v. Gore*, 531 U.S. 98 (2000). Whatever one's view of the merits of the election and of the judicial case, there was at stake here the integrity of the electoral process itself, raising the question whether, and in what sense we live in a democracy. I would have thought nothing would have engendered more alarm and criticism and conversation than such a crisis, especially among lawyers. (Compare the popular resistance seen in Mexico at that time to a challenged national election.)

survive in a world in which equality is systematically denied by such disparities of wealth and power. Under these conditions the best we can have is a series of contests among the powerful, sometimes resolved by plebiscites.

I believe we have become to a large degree the subjects of an oligarchy, a sort of internal empire. By empire here I do not mean merely the cultural forces, strong as they are, that make up what Simone Weil calls an "empire of force,"[8] but an actual political reality in which unelected people rule much of our lives. Their main object seems to be to extract as much economic value as possible from the earth and the oceans and the air, and from the labor—and unemployment—of billions of people.

This empire has co-opted many of us—perhaps all of us who read this book—who might be its critics, because we to a large degree benefit, though in a relatively small way, by the same policies that enrich the super-rich. We eat at expensive restaurants, and take trips to Europe, and buy expensive suits. So do the reporters for the *Washington Post* and the *New York Times*. There is in our world almost no real voice for the poor, which is perhaps a third of our nation. The *New York Times* does of course take positions of concern for the poor on its editorial pages. But its sections on "Arts and Leisure and Style," let alone "Travel & Escapes" and the advertising in its Sunday magazine, all with one voice affirm the value of wealth and consumption and the world of radical inequality they create.

Under the present administration the tendencies I describe have accelerated and taken a new form: the emergence of a national regime that seems to have little or no respect for law or democracy as we have been talking about them in this book. It is an empire of a new kind in this country. There are forces that resist it, but there is no way of telling how this contest will come out.

But we seemed simply to accept what we were told, as if it did not matter much to us. I include most law schools and law teachers in that "we." Of course there were some articles on the subject, but I hardly heard the matter discussed, and certainly not as an important matter on which we as lawyers and law teachers had a special responsibility to speak. Why was this? Was it because in a deep sense we did not think we had a democracy any longer?

8. In her wonderful sentence: "Il n'est pas possible d'aimer et d'être juste que si l'on connaît l'empire de la force et si l'on sait ne pas le respecter," or in English: "No one can love and be just who does not understand the empire of force and know how not to respect it." See her "L'Iliade ou la poème de la force," *Cahiers du Sud* (December 1940–January 1941).

Democracy at Work

Having painted this distressing picture, I want to say that in my experience there is a remarkable force of another and opposed kind in American life — not much seen in the media or in the world of national politics — which I would call a natural readiness for self-government. It is regrettably not universal in our country, but I believe it is very widespread. We see it in local politics all the time, in elections for the school board say, and in homeowner associations and other private groups. This is the world where we know how to create an organization — with president, vice president, treasurer, secretary — which is subject to bylaws and a statement of purpose, and whose meetings follow Robert's Rules of Order. We know how to live in the space it defines: how to hold meetings and reach decisions and live with them even when we disagree; how to define our common values and purposes and try to live by them.

But this capacity for self-government — perhaps our greatest national treasure — is simply not much visible either in the ways I see the nation described in the media nor in the ways politicians and officials talk about it nor in the way I see the national government functioning. Congress, for example, does not work as I describe the school board working, in a real way, with real debates, and real decisions: all too often it seems to be only an image or phantasm of itself, a pretense of government, in which almost nothing is ever said that anyone means. What one hears is almost always calculated and shaped, as a piece of advertising is shaped, by asking what will work with the audience one is simultaneously flattering and manipulating. This is sometimes even true of judicial opinions.

The Disappearance of Law

My second phenomenon — perhaps you perceive it too — is the experience of reading certain Supreme Court opinions which seem evidently written by clerks and not much rewritten by the justices.[9] These opinions seem to speak in no one's voice, without seriousness, without a sense of responsibility for what is done or said, as though deciding the case and

9. I should say that what I describe here is an impression, not a verifiable fact. And I do not include all opinions or all justices in this criticism. Justice Souter in particular seemed to me to adhere to high standards of legal thinking and judging. Likewise, I do not mean

explaining the decision were empty exercises. Related to this phenomenon is another, which is the loss of the very idea that one could admire a judge with whom, or an opinion with which, one disagreed.

The Courts and the Law Schools

The opinions I describe do not seem to me in any way to reflect, as I was taught an opinion should, a deep struggle to determine the meaning of the relevant legal authorities—and in the process to find one's own mind growing and learning—but rather to express a largely unexamined judgment one way or the other as to the result of the case, often based on rather crude previous commitments of a political kind, which are not tested in the crucible of thought and argument.[10] This kind of formulaic jurisprudence does not expose the true reasons and thinking of the Court, and subject it to criticism; and it does not produce texts that can be read with the kind of care and attention we are used to giving texts in the law, as I have tried to do in the earlier chapters of this book.

The Supreme Court may even be losing its character as a Court, with some of the Justices simply carrying out an ideology which their opinions are designed to defend, rather than engaging on the merits in an

---

to criticize the clerks by what I say: they are not deciding the cases and cannot be expected to explain with any authenticity why someone else is doing so. All they can do is what they do, which is to produce a set of canned arguments, like those in a typical law review note, in such a way as to tilt the balance in the direction their Justice has ordered. If I am right in my sense of the kind of "law" being made at the highest levels, this means that the kind of criticism of judicial opinions, positive and negative, that I and many others have engaged in over the years is no longer possible. There will be no such thing as a good or bad opinion, only a raw decision to like or not like.

Recent news tells us that there has been an effort by the Federalist Society to train people appointed as clerks in the ideas and rhetorical moves of what is called "conservatism."

10. For one example, see the opinion of the Court in *Free Speech Coalition v. United States*, 535 U.S. 234 (2002), discussed in *Living Speech: Resisting the Empire of Force*, 143–60 (2006). This opinion, by Justice Kennedy, seems to me very poor; but some of his other work was distinguished, especially the joint opinion in *Planned Parenthood v. Casey*, 505 U.S. 833 (1992), written with Justices Souter and O'Connor. This opinion is analyzed in *Acts of Hope: Creating Authority in Literature, Law, and Politics*, 153–86 (1994).

I also want to mention the bombastic and bullying tone of some opinions, full of self-certain contempt for those who think differently, which seem to me deliberately destructive of the civility that is necessary to the functioning of a truly collegial court or other institution. Both kinds of opinions seem to me to move in the direction of abandoning a central principle of law, the principle of responsibility.

open-minded way that might lead them and us to better ways of understanding and of being. It is essential to honest judicial work that the judge come to every case with as open a mind as he or she can manage, ready to listen to the arguments each way, on their merits, and prepared in doing so to see the case in a new light. Our two most recent Supreme Court appointments, Justices Gorsuch and Kavanaugh, perhaps against their own wishes, have been proposed and resisted, so far as appears in the public discourse, on the grounds that they will decide certain cases in certain ways. In the process of confirmation there was, so far as I know at least, no talk about the merits of open-mindedness and intellectual honesty—the core of judicial ethics and the heart of judicial independence.

For a comparison, let me suggest you look through a volume of Supreme Court reports from forty or fifty years ago. The difference to me is striking: here we have distinctive voices, distinctive minds working seriously, responding to each other, trying to say the truth as they see it. Of course they are subject to frailty and bias, as we all are, and I do not want to sentimentalize their work, but at their best they are engaged in a process of self-education, and the education of the public as well. Just to list the names is to invoke a different world. In 1962, for example, when I was in law school the Justices were Black, Frankfurter, Douglas, Clark, Warren, Harlan, Brennan, Stewart, and White, all highly respectable people by any measure. I can myself remember turning to the cases of this era with interest and enthusiasm as I no longer can do.

I also see a turning away from the law in law schools themselves, which seem to me to have to some degree become closer to "think tanks" or public policy institutes than the schools of professional training I once knew. In casebooks the cases seem often to be reduced to paradigms meant to facilitate argument about theory, rather than seen, as they occur in practice, as complex challenges to the mind, in which law interacts with facts, facts with law, different laws with different laws, and all these things with our developing sense of justice. Rather, the main interest seems to be in questions of policy and theory abstracted from the life of the law.

I was taught that the central legal questions, for lawyer and judge alike, are these: What texts should count as authoritative, and why? What do they mean, and why? What weight should be given to the judgment a text reflects, and why? How in the light of all these things, and in the context of the present, including the facts of the case, should the case be decided? Of course I knew that lawyers would disagree on the merits of all these questions, but I believed they should agree in affirming a world in which power is distributed, regulated, reviewed.

The academic tendency I mean is manifest perhaps particularly in what is called "law and economics," but not only there. It runs through some of the ways in which scholarship is evaluated and it shows up in our almost total silence about law teaching. When I went into law teaching it was with great doubt about whether I would ever write anything, but with great confidence that the teaching of law was itself an activity—an art with a meaning—that could occupy a mind and justify a life. I wonder if anyone thinks that today.

A system of policy critique of the kind that is at work in our law schools may make useful discoveries, but such a system cannot perform the functions of law itself. Neither economics nor sociology nor psychology nor any other field can address, let alone resolve, the distinctive legal questions about the identity and meaning of authoritative texts and about the degree of deference due the judgments of others.[11] Taking economics as my example—though the same point could be made about any other field—I would say: One cannot do law in the language of economics, or economics in the language of the law. To try to do either would be as ludicrous as trying to do science in the language of religion, or religion in the language of science.[12]

---

11. My colleague Philip Soper has built a whole ethical theory upon what he learned from the law's practices of deference. See his *An Ethics of Deference* (2002).

12. Not to say that there is no place for economics, or other disciplines, in the law. Of course there is, as I suggested in chapter four, whenever the discipline in question has something to teach the law, which is very often indeed, from the use of expert testimony on questions of engineering, for example, to the use of psychology to illuminate antisocial conduct or the nature of insanity, to the use of sociology to demonstrate the existence of social conditions that call for our response. But in no case can the language of the external discipline substitute for that of the law; it must be translated into it, an activity that requires its own complex art.

What economics should do is to accept and welcome its place as one language among many, one way of thinking among many, each of which has its own contribution to make. A central task in addressing any serious problem is that of assessing the resources and limits of each available method. In the law, it is the law that has this task, just as in history it is history, in psychology psychology, and so on. The problem of economics as practiced

Cost-Benefit Analysis

My sense of what I mean by the loss of law is well exemplified in two brief passages by Judge Richard A. Posner. In the first, Judge Posner is writing in favor of what he calls "pragmatism," meaning the decision of legal cases by a judicial balancing of costs and benefits. The only reason for attending to prior legal texts, in his view, is that to disregard them would have social costs, and these costs should be taken into account by the person with power.

> The point is not that the judge has some kind of moral or even political duty to abide by constitutional or statutory text, or by precedent; that would be formalism. It is merely that continuity and restraint in the judicial function are important social goods, and any judge proposing to innovate must consider not only the benefits of the innovation but also the costs in injury to those goods.[13]

To me this misunderstands the nature of both law and democracy, including the obligation—moral, political, and legal—to respect the authority of legal texts and the fundamental principle of separation of powers. In the world called into being by this passage law would lose its essential meaning.

Similarly, in a letter to the *New York Review of Books*, responding to a critical review by Professor David Cole of his book *Not a Suicide Pact*, Judge Posner said that Cole must realize that his civil libertarian principles

> are not the product of "text, tradition, and reason" since equally capable legal thinkers hold opposite views. This is possible because there is no consensus on what methodology to use to resolve constitutional disputes and because text, tradition, precedent, and reason so often tug in different directions. . . . Realism requires recognition that constitutional decision-making at the highest level (The US Supreme Court) in the most difficult cases is driven in the main by policy judgments based usually on just the kind of balancing that Cole

---

in law schools is in this sense a problem of writing and translation. For elaboration of this point, see *Justice as Translation*, 76–79 (1990).

13. Richard A. Posner, "Pragmatism versus Purposivism in First Amendment Analysis," 54 *Stanford Law Review* 737, 739 (2002).

> deplores. Or pretends to deplore; for I imagine *au fond* the reason he dislikes the administration's counterterrorism measures is that he thinks they impose greater costs, in harm to civil liberties, than the benefits they confer in reducing the risk of further terrorist attacks. The rest is rhetoric.[14]

This passage adds to the misunderstanding expressed in the first. Together they represent with great clarity the state of affairs I am trying to define in this chapter and in the book as a whole. Of course the meaning of the authoritative texts of the law is often highly arguable in a range of cases. But that does not mean that we can dismiss them as useless, or that in the zone of disagreement we are free to apply whatever version of cost benefit analysis, or other method or theory, happens to appeal to us. What Posner contemptuously dismisses as "rhetoric" is nothing less than the entire world of law: its structure of authority, its democratic basis, its creation of a constituted government based upon separation of powers. In its place he proposes a view that all that matters is power, a view in which not only is there no need to respect the opinion of another, there is no way in which this can be done.

Indeed there is something deeply incoherent in Posner's view, for how is the question to be answered, whose calculation of costs and benefits is to count? Apparently the judge's; but why? The position of power that the judge occupies, and which Posner assumes, does not itself reflect somebody's present judgment of costs and benefits, but rests upon law in the sense in which I have been describing it: it is an instance of the democratic allocation of function to decide, within limits and subject to guidance and review.

What Law Can Be

I have a sense, then, that law itself is being eroded and transformed, just as I said earlier democracy is being eroded and transformed, and in both cases in the service of what I have called the empire, that is, a system of power that does not respect democracy or law. This fact has a tragic quality because the law by its nature should be a strong force of resistance to the principles of empire, a strong force of defense for democracy.

---

14. Richard A Posner, "Letter to the Editor," *New York Review of Books,* January 11, 2007, page 63.

For the law is built at its foundations upon the principle of separation of powers, not their merger into a single force. In this it is the opposite of empire. In our law every institutional actor must acknowledge and respect judgments made by others: the legislature must respect the judgments expressed in the Constitution, the courts the judgments of the legislature, lower courts the judgment of higher courts, and so on. This means that the lawyer never addresses a person who has all the power. Both lawyer and judge constantly turn to other texts, composed by other persons, who have made judgments which they are bound to respect.

It is crucial that the texts that our law invokes as authoritative, and to which the judges and lawyers pay respect or deference, all rest in some way upon the authority of democratic institutions. They are statutes passed by elected legislatures, or opinions issued by judges appointed by elected governors, or contracts written by the parties themselves, and so on. In affirming the value and validity of its own processes our law is thus always affirming democracy.[15]

The law is not a closed system, operating behind locked doors, but is connected in hundreds of ways to our democratic culture. To disregard this structure of authority, and to replace it with a theory—whether philosophical, political, or economic in kind—let alone with an ideology of pure power itself, is to erode our democracy at the root. For in the world of theory the rightness of the result depends upon its congruence with the theory in question, necessarily a theory without any basis in democratic authority but resting solely upon the commitments of those who are persuaded by it: the community of believers. In the world of pure power, the only thing that matters is what the powerful want.

At the simplest level, what the law teaches is that we live in a world in which different people can have different, decent, and reasonable views;

15. As we saw in chapter four, the law is a system of thought and language that is open to, and in tension with, other systems, in principle to all others, and is in this way as well deeply democratic in nature. In any legal case a whole field of knowledge and expertise may become relevant, from engineering to sociology or psychology to history or medicine. The law is committed to learning what it can from these systems of knowledge. Likewise, especially under our jury system, our law has a commitment to the validity and value of ordinary language, the language of the citizen as such, for it must always be ready to be translated into that language, particularly in jury instructions and in closing arguments. The awareness that at some time the law will have to make sense to ordinary people is a discipline that tends to erode what might otherwise be a hermetically sealed overconfidence in its specialized vocabulary.

that we need a way to respect these views and judge among them fairly, that is, openly and honestly; that the world constructed by the law is one that distributes the power to decide such questions differentially to various public and private agents—so that even if we lose this case, or this issue, we have a residue of autonomy and freedom and a real reason to remain faithful to the law as such; and that all this being true we cannot fairly and rightly decide disputes by reference to theory, or our own estimate of costs and benefits, or to the sorts of clichés and buzzwords and slogans that characterize much political talk. The law, at its best, improves our thought and our language.

What has been happening to law, however, is that it is becoming an instrument of empire and power, and in the process losing its essential character.

Dehumanization

My third phenomenon is the dehumanization of human beings. There are many ways in which this phenomenon is on the rise, but I shall deal mainly with a rather pure and self-conscious form of it, namely, our deliberate and systematic torture of people to extract information from them and the effort to justify this practice.

This question came to the forefront in response to the efforts of the second Bush administration to legalize what any sensible person would call "torture"—certainly if he or she were subjected to it—and the related effort to remove from all protections of the law a class of human beings selected by officials as "enemy combatants." At the time I was surprised by how weak and unfocussed resistance seemed to be. Of course there were honorable exceptions in the bar and in the public world, but there was not what there should have been, a universal public outcry of a sort that would have driven the beast of torture off the field of our shared life. My concern about this issue has been sharpened by the 2018 appointment of Gina Haspel—deeply involved as she was in the torture program of the Bush administration—as head of the CIA, an appointment that has been tolerated by Congress and the public in a way that is deeply disturbing.

The issue of torture has haunted me more than anything else. Not so much because American soldiers have on occasion beaten, abused, tortured, and killed people they have captured. Those are terrible things, but war always includes them, just as it includes the incineration of little children, the rape of women, the purposive destruction of life itself. What is new here are the efforts to make torture and cruelty part of the approved business of government, claiming for it the authority of law, and to establish the existence of a class of persons under the control of the government who are completely beyond any protection of law.[16]

To connect this image with what I said about the state of legal thinking, I think we hear an all too familiar voice in the famous "torture memorandum": it is written in mechanical and conclusory terms, as though a routine legal analysis of a rather empty kind could simply be used without thought and without question to justify human torture.[17] There is no sense of a person in the prose, no one making judgments for which he is responsible. It troubles me to think, as I do, that this is a voice for which we who teach in law schools may be especially responsible.

With respect to the cruelty our government has shown towards immigrants and their children we have not been given even a memorandum purporting to justify it. It rests upon pure power, including both the power to hide and deny the truth and the power to stimulate hostility towards the disfavored human beings by propaganda. It is an effort to put its victims outside the law entirely.

The Propaganda of Torture

Part of the reason for our supine lack of response to torture is our habituation to the sort of advertising and propaganda I have mentioned, for which the fears generated by the events of 9/11, and stimulated since, provide strong nourishment. According to this thin and inadequate form of thinking, there is an ineradicable line between "us"—the good people of America, under unjustified and aggressive threat—and "them,"

16. In recent years we have seen official dehumanization of an analogous kind, namely, of refugees and asylum seekers along our southern border, and especially of their children, who have first been callously removed from their parents, then, in many cases, simply lost track of. To remove a child from his or her parents, especially a young one, is to inflict on him or her a torture of the soul. This is done either for convenience' sake or, in my view more likely, as part of a program to normalize official brutality and cruelty.

17. Jay S. Bybee, "Memorandum for Alberto Gonzalez, counsel to the President, Re: Standards of Conduct for Interrogation under 18 U.S.C. Sections 2340–2340A," August 1, 2002, in Mark Danner, *Torture and Truth: America, Abu Graib, and the War on Terror* (2004). For a fine analysis of the issues addressed, and not addressed, in this memorandum, see Jose Alvarez, "Torturing the Law," 37 *Case Western Reserve Journal of International Law* 175 (2006).

those others, whose torture or "severe interrogation" is in question. Why should we care about what happens to them? They are the enemy, or at least irredeemably "other."[18]

But of course they are not these things in fact: they are fellow human beings, some of them citizens of our country; they are selected for torture or abuse not by some foolproof process that will identify without error the "bad," whoever they are, but by who knows whom, acting on who knows what information, and with who knows what motives, with all this happening behind a deliberate screen of secrecy.[19]

The central principle of democratic government is official responsibility to the public, and here that is entirely erased. No one stands up as the one who has made the crucial decisions; no one in the public even knows that most of them have been made.

The fate of Guantanamo prisoners who were returned to their own countries is instructive: apparently almost all of them were released after investigation by their home governments, it turning out that many of them had been seized without any justification at all by persons seeking a bounty offered for the identification of "terrorists." Only a handful were tried in their home countries and at least by 2006 none of those had been convicted of any crime.[20]

Even if someone is in fact an "enemy," that of course does not justify his torture. Maybe he has to be killed, if he is shooting at you, but when captured he should be treated humanely and with dignity, as we hope our soldiers will be treated when they are captured.

"The Need for Information"

It is sometimes argued that torture is justified by the need for "information." This argument works by another specious form of thought, which, when added to the first, seeks to establish a sense of necessity that will remove torture from the moral sphere almost completely. The form of thought I mean is captured in this question, repeated endlessly in the media, and even in classrooms: "If you knew that there was an atom

---

18. On the deliberate killing of American citizens abroad by presidential order see Jefferson Powell, *Targeting Americans: The Constitutionality of the U.S. Drone War* (2016).

19. A similar secrecy marks the abuse of children at the border, especially when they are removed to unknown sites and subject to who knows what abuse by what unknown and unknowable people.

20. See *Detroit Free Press*, December 16, 2006, page 6A, story by Andrew O. Skelsky.

bomb somewhere downtown with a timer ticking wouldn't you torture the people who knew about it to make them tell you where it was, or how to disarm it?"

The question seems to pose a serious problem of moral thought, but, like many such hypotheticals, it is not real. You can never "know" there is an atom bomb, or a timer ticking; and you can never "know" that you have one of the "people who know about it." The facts assumed by the hypothetical never exist in any individual case. And even if there were one such case that would do nothing to justify the hundreds or thousands or tens of thousands of cases in which we have engaged in torture. The question about the ticking bomb invites us to live in a false world—the world ultimately of advertising and propaganda—not the real world.

The unreal hypothetical is used not to support the proposition that it might possibly support, namely that in a wildly rare and dramatic case one would use torture, but something very different, namely that torture itself should be evaluated simply by weighing the costs and benefits of the practice. "You believe in torture in one case in a million," we are being told, "therefore you can have no objection to our regular use of torture as an instrument of policy, under whatever procedures and standards we choose."

The logic of cost-benefit analysis is epitomized in the ticking bomb case, but it runs far more widely and deeply in our culture than that hypothetical. All of the practices of abuse and inhumanity, including the abuses at the border, rest upon the same claim, that "national security" or the "safety of the nation" require it, an invocation of "cost-benefit analysis" that often reflects no analysis whatever.

Irrationality

Despite its claims to a high degree of rationality, the kind of cost-benefit analysis that is so often offered as an alternative to legal thought in fact tends not to be rational but irrational.[21] It is a long-standing truism in the critique of "balancing," for example, that the outcome is often determined by the way in which the interests are articulated. Are we to define

21. In this context I would like to call attention to one of the most systematic and extensive efforts to use cost-benefit analysis to decide what to do about a social problem, namely the *Report of the Third London Airport Commission* (1971). The question was where the third

the question as "the safety of the nation" versus "this person's desire to keep this piece of information to himself"? Or as "the importance of privacy and freedom of speech" versus "the utility of this particular piece of information to the government"? The outcome-shaping characterization is of course often driven by desire, perhaps unconscious desire, for a certain result. In this sense the designation of costs and benefits, seemingly so rational, is often in the end not rational at all, but a mere pretense.

Who, after all, is to quantify the danger that terrorism presents? The incantation of the phrase "national security" is offered as a universal acid that will erase everything except the fear that it stimulates. This

---

major airport near London should be located, and the matter was subject to exhaustive analysis of social costs and benefits. To the extent possible these were not determined by fiat, but by market transactions, which were used to establish the cost of travel time to the West End, the value of green spaces to a local community, and so on. They concluded that the airport should be located in the only green area between London and Birmingham. This result depended, as the dissenter pointed out, upon a particular calculation of the value of travel time, which if modified only slightly would have sent the airport to estuary lands east of London.

So which calculation was right? And how do you determine the value of green land to a neighboring community, or of a Norman church to be destroyed by the bulldozers? The study was defective in another way, the dissent argued, for it failed entirely to address the social benefits of locating the airport to the east that would arise from investment and expenditure in this relatively poor area, and contribute at least in some measure to the righting of the imbalance between East London and West London. What the majority said in response amounted an expression of fear, that the longer travel time to the eastern location might lead American travel agents, for such there existed in those days, to skip England altogether and pour their customers, and their money, into Germany or France—a fear that was not given a number, as could not rationally have been done. The final fillip is that, as you may know from your own experience of flying to London, it was finally decided that there was no need for such an airport at all. (Actually, in recent years the airport at Stansted, one of the original candidates, has been more widely used, I think mainly for European travel.)

In the context of what faces us today, this kind of analysis may lead, as perhaps it has, to conduct that is not only immoral and wrong, as is the torture carried out by our government or with its consent, but, in addition, to conduct that will have the opposite effect of that intended, that is, not to produce new information that will make us safer, but in effect to recruit hostile agents, which will of course make us less safe. In fact our torture and abuse may indeed already have done this. All this is done in the name of national security, but it may well be that our lawlessness is making us less secure, not more—as well as having the "social cost" of turning us into a nation that tortures. (Unless the real reason for the program of torture is not to get information at all, but to define us as a lawless and torturing nation in the hopes that this will make people fear us.) For more on this Report see *The Legal Imagination* 700–06 (1973, 2018).

talk about overwhelming necessity fails to address the obvious questions—obvious to a lawyer, that is: Who shall determine whether such a necessity exists? Under what procedures and standards? Subject to what review? These are the core questions of legal thought, and they are by this logic erased. For to take those questions seriously would be to invoke the whole apparatus of law as we know it, and that will not be allowed.

It will not be allowed for another reason, I think, namely, that torture cannot in the end be legalized: it cannot bear the light of day, but must go on behind locked doors in unmarked buildings, in mysterious and unknown places reached by darkened airplanes, and carried out by anonymous interrogators and their anonymous assistants.[22] The cost-benefit analysis must not include, because it cannot do so, the reality of the torture itself and the evil it does to the tortured and to the torturers alike.

The corrosive effect of "cost-benefit analysis" here is even worse than I have said. The question presented by the ticking bomb case is whether the "known" existence of the ticking bomb justified torture. But of course such a bomb may in fact exist though unsuspected by us; if so, it presents in fact exactly the same real-world danger as if it were known; does that not justify the use of what is euphemistically called "extreme measures" to find out? Indeed anyone may know *something* that is of comparable value, perhaps without even knowing how important it is. The true need for information is potentially just as great in those cases as in the ticking bomb case itself. To think in terms of a single value that outweighs all others, here "national security," is a form not of rationality but irrationality, ultimately a kind of insanity.[23]

The logic at work here leads to universal spying, universal wiretapping, universal torture, limited only by whatever costs are perceived by the perpetrator—or, more accurately, by the superior officer who in the comfort of his or her own office orders the perpetrator to torture. And this line of thinking not only justifies torture, it would justify anything.

---

22. It is for this reason I think that the children separated from their parents at the border, and other immigrant children as well, have been isolated from the media and other visitors. If photos and videos and soundtracks of these children were readily available, I think the practices would have to stop.

23. *Dennis v. United States*, 341 U.S. 494 (1951), shows this process at work.

It erases not only protective legal rules, but the inherent protections of legal thought itself.

Once you start on a process of interest balancing in which one of the items is of potentially infinite value you have committed yourself to an impossible world of paranoia, not law—a world like the world of human slavery—in which one value cancels all others, in which appetite, as Shakespeare says, becomes a universal wolf and at last eats up itself.[24]

Human Slavery

Of course this is not the only time in our history that people have tried to use our law for terrible purposes, as chapter three makes plain. What I do not say in that chapter is that one effect of the use of the law to enforce our practice of human slavery, one of the greatest crimes in history, was to destroy the integrity of law itself—and obviously democracy as well—in ways that are relevant to our present situation. It is of course obvious that slavery destroyed the idea of democracy in the slave states, for the core of democracy is legal equality. My concern here is with what happened to the law under these conditions.

My first exposure to the law of human slavery came many years ago, when I was thinking about the difficulty of using the American language of race in the law, or anywhere else for that matter—an effort that culminated in chapter four above.

I had the idea of seeing what the law of slavery was like and went to

24. *Troilus and Cressida*, act I, scene 3, line 124. I mention slavery because something similar to it is at work in the logic of the torture cases, including a repudiation of the essential principle that our law is neutral as to persons. We now have, in so-called "enemy combatants," a class of persons who are not persons under the law, and are without a right to lawyers, judges, appearances in court, without a right to any regular proceeding presided over by a neutral judge, in which they can see and question the evidence against them. They may be tortured or killed, in the government's view, without any recourse other than that which happens to be afforded, or not, by the administration in its mercy. This is an image of power that it profoundly imperial, restoring at a stroke a vision of a king beyond law that precedes the Magna Carta, a vision that in fact may have no formal antecedents in European or American history except those of the totalitarian states of the twentieth century. These people are "enemy combatants" because some unnamed person, on the basis of unrevealed evidence or rumor, has decided they are. They are the juridical equivalent of slaves, but without even the few protections granted by the law of Mississippi or Alabama, or by the society at large. Much the same status is now put upon the people at the border, including children.

the basement of the library, where I found the Alabama session laws, arrayed from the beginning to the current year. I walked back along them until I found 1833, took the volume down, and looked up slavery in the index. And there it was: our legal system used to create and perpetuate a hideous system of cruelty, inhumanity, and degradation.

I was horrified, and for the first time faced the question: Is our law simply a neutral instrument that can be used for any purpose whatever—torture, slavery, genocide? Or does it have some enduring principles of respect for human dignity, for the integrity and value of the human person and personality, which means that when it is used for such purposes it is being profoundly abused—and abused in ways that are manifest in the reasoning and writing that achieve such things, making them not really law at all, but a kind of perversion or parody of law? I came to the conclusion that when law was used to perpetuate and manage human slavery, it became something else, and foreign, not really law. The premises of legal reasoning were erased as the whole system came to serve ultimately a single value, that of racial domination.

One of these premises is the idea of consistency in the meaning and application of the law. The law had to have a way of imagining the human beings it called slaves, and what was that? As property, part of the law said. But if that were applied consistently, slaves would be incapable of crime. But when they were charged with crime, they were no longer property, but people. And sometimes they were imagined as animals. What explained the shift from one way of thinking and imagining to the other? It was perfectly obvious: the law would speak in whatever way most disadvantaged the slave. This is not how law, as law, functions.

The issue is not merely formal consistency. Equally important is the way the law normally treats conflicts of value, namely, by recognizing the conflict, seeing something to be said on both sides, and then striking a balance in a particular case, now one way, now another. Think for example of the field of criminal procedure which has the tension at its center between the legitimate needs of law enforcement and the important rights of persons suspected of, or charged with, crime. The law pricks out a line between the two poles in conflict, always seeking rationality and consistency, though of course never attaining them.

But in slave law, the subjugation of human beings by law and public force outweighed all other values. Law became a single value system. This is so inconsistent with its nature that in an important sense it was no longer law at all. As a lawyer in that system one could not have thought and spoken and argued as one does in our law.

The topic of justice, central to our idea of law, could not be authentically invoked in such a system, because one thing we mean by justice is a fundamental equality before the law. This is a point where law and democracy in our world come close to being the same thing. You may be poor, but you are entitled to make a claim against a rich person, or a corporation, and have it listened to with respect and attention. Under the regime of human slavery, millions of people, slaves and "free blacks" alike, were denied his most fundamental of legal rights. They were not persons in the law.

At the heart of our law is the principle that courts are open to everyone, and that any person can make the claim that the law give him or her a right. Any person can in principle tell the story of his life and claim meaning for it in the language of the law. Of course you can sometimes lose, but you can be heard. But the slave could not be heard, and after *Dred Scott* the African American could not be heard. This silencing of the abused and degraded person in a deep way rendered the law of slavery no law at all.

I say this about slavery because something similar is at work in the logic of the torture cases. We now have a class of persons who are not persons under the law.[25]

Democracy and Empire

The spring from which I think all these evils flow, including our incapacity to resist them, is the fact that at some level we know that we in this country are subjects of an empire committed to rule by force and propaganda—and an external empire, as well as the internal one I described earlier. This external empire works in a new way for our country, at least on this scale, that is not by influencing international institutions and agreements, not through the management of global trade, but by threat and extortion, to the damage of trade and to the movement of people. Not by law but by force.

---

25. For more on slave law and what came after it, see *The Legal Imagination*, 430–503 (1973, 2018)

We know, I think rightly, that it is not possible for an empire of either kind to respect the assumptions and aspirations of democracy under law. The very idea and existence of the empire depends upon a line between "us" and "them"—those who count as the "we," the rulers who have the power, and "they," including our own citizens, the ruled, who are subject to it. In the eyes of the empire the ordinary people of this country have no different status from foreign nationals: all are subject to the same imperial and dictatorial regime. Our nation is on its way to becoming a third-world country politically as well as economically.

But the fact that we have become an imperial nation, internally and externally, is something it is hard to admit, for it contradicts our deepest principles. It is I think at bottom our need to deny the fact of empire that makes us so ready to submit ourselves and our judgments to slogans, clichés, and falsehoods—to live in the false world of political advertising and propaganda.

This perception about empire, if I am right, connects my three themes: the concentration of wealth in the hands of the few, the transformations in what we mean by law, and the acceptance of dehumanization, particularly in the instance of torture.

If the antidemocratic principles necessary to the functioning of the empire are inconsistent with law, we are implicitly told or shown, law itself must change its character. To try either to be democratic at home and function as an empire abroad, or to function as an empire at home and try to be democratic in our foreign relations, would make a mockery of the principles of equality and justice under law that are essential to what we mean by democracy. An empire by its nature denies the fundamental principle of human equality and requires dominance and subjugation, wherever it reaches, and in doing so necessarily erodes the idea and reality of law.

Although this is not often said, I think that one implicit argument in support of the subjugating power of the empire, in both its forms, is that the simple fact of an immense power imbalance not only justifies empire but requires it. The rich and the superrich—individuals and corporations alike—are so powerful that we cannot imagine any effective way of demanding fairness from them or insisting upon equality with them, at home or abroad. In both cases the fact of gross disparity overwhelms the hope of equality by declaring it impossible.

This argument in favor of the empire is a modern version of a very old argument, articulated (and rejected) by both Plato and Thucydides, namely that justice is a proper topic of thought and argument only among equals. Thus Thucydides in the famous Melian Dialogue has the Athenians tell their victims—the people of Melos who had rebelled against them—that where there is great disparity of power, those who have it will do whatever they want; the rest must submit or die, and there is no point in pretending otherwise. In this way the Athenians seek to explain their refusal to recognize any constraint upon their power to kill and enslave all those who have rebelled against them. They claim to be beyond the reach of justice or its language.

The Athenians say they are willing to listen to the Melians, not on the subject of what justice requires, for that is irrelevant to them, but upon considerations of self-interest only. This in fact does not leave the Melians with nothing to say: they tell the Athenians, for example, that though they are powerful now, the time may come when they will want to invoke considerations of justice. If they reject them now, they will not be able to do so later, for they will have defined themselves as outlaws. Likewise, in not respecting the neutrality of the Melians, the Athenians are at a stroke destroying the difference between enemy and neutral, and thus making enemies of all the world. Athens rejects these arguments, and destroys Melos.

The Melians are proven right. Athens undertakes the foolish and impossible expedition against Sicily in part because it has no way of thinking sensibly about its real interests and how to pursue them. In particular it no longer has the use of the language of international law, which defined the city-states and their relations and in doing so had made Athens' earlier achievements both possible and meaningful. It was the existence and working of that law that enabled Athens to engage in the sensible definition and pursuit of its interests. But having won at the game of international competition for power, Athens destroys the game itself, leaving itself without any way of imagining the world in which it functions. Under these circumstances Athens has no way to be rational.

In Sicily Athens is defeated—leading ultimately to the destruction of its power, to its occupation by the Spartans, and to the temporary end of its democracy—in part because, when it discovers that it needs an alliance, those whom they approach refuse them, regarding Athens as having rejected the system it is trying to invoke.

Such are the consequences of Athens' insistence upon its imperial superiority to justice and law. It is a hard story with a plain moral for our day.

Thucydides makes the story even harder, however, for from what he says it is not clear that Athens *could* have effectively invoked and complied with the conventions of international law at Melos, even if it had wanted to. If they made a treaty, for example, would not the other party feel free to disregard it, knowing that they could always claim that the treaty was coerced? Maybe, then, it is not Athens' stupidity or viciousness that is at work in Melos and beyond, but a recognition that its extraordinary power in fact does remove it from the world of law and justice. It is not to its own advantage, but this is what their power does. Under one reading of Thucydides, this is what it means to have an empire.[26]

I see in our own empire a claim similar to that of Athens—externally, on behalf of the nation with respect to other nations; internally, on behalf of the rich with respect to our own people. The very fact of power of this scale and magnitude is implicitly said to make law and democracy impossible; and, as I have been arguing in this chapter, we tend to submit to the claim, without quite knowing that we do so.

Is what was true of Athens true of us? Are we unable to escape from the lawlessness and injustice of empire? Thucydides has no advice, except by implication not to form an empire in the first place. But I think we do have a response, thanks to the invention over centuries of what we call equality under law, the premise that in the courtroom differences of race, gender, wealth, and class should, at least for the moment, disappear. Each party should have an equal opportunity to speak to the merits of the case, which alone should determine the outcome. Of course this ideal is never fully achieved, but it is alive in our minds as a principle and as a ground of criticism and self-correction. It may be possible at least in this sense to create an equality we do not find.

I think our task as lawyers and judges and teachers and citizens, within our country, is to insist upon the value of law and legal thought, and of the democracy they express and make possible; abroad, it is to recognize that as our military and economic power increases it becomes increasingly important to our interests, and to our existence, that here too we recognize and respect the value of the law—a recognition and respect that are all the more important if not compelled but chosen. In the international sphere the law can create something of an equality of states, and in that sense of persons, even where there is no equality of wealth

26. For more on Thucydides see *When Words Lose Their Meaning*, chapter three (1984).

and power. Internally, within our own country we can work towards a substantive equality as well, that is an equal access to the essentials of human thriving. The premises of democracy require no less.

In both cases, at home and abroad, it is in a revival of the law that we have our brightest hope.

The history I have recounted teaches us that where there are immense imbalances of power, within our country or in the larger world, the powerful should not reject with contempt the claims of law and justice, as the Athenians did, but do quite the reverse. It is precisely at the point where one nation or group has the power to disregard such claims that it is most important, for the powerful themselves and for the rest of the world, that they cheerfully submit to them. For against the inequalities of wealth and power that are so often part of the human condition the law can create a kind of equality of its own, imperfect but real—what we call equality under law.

In the end, it is not just the weak who need the rule of law and the claims of justice; all of us do.

It is obvious that the movement away from law and democracy that I describe in the chapter has continued and intensified since it was first written. I would no longer say that our talk of law and democracy hides the fact that we are subject to an internal empire. That fact is too plain to be missed by anyone. It is not just an empire run by large corporations, however, using the language of economics to explain itself; rather, it seems to represent a political movement that has no respect for the Constitution or laws or traditions of the country and is eager to dismantle these things.

In particular we face a political force that wants to dehumanize members of races other than the "white" race. If the dreams of this movement are fulfilled it might well mean the end of both law and democracy.

How can we live as responsible citizens under this threat? That is the question of my last chapter.

6

Difficulty and Responsibility in the Face of Evil

How do we begin to live, to imagine ourselves into existence, in a world like the one described in chapter five? We already live in an empire, one that may well be evolving into an unconstitutional and unlawful rule.[1] *What can we do about that, beyond lamenting it? Can we keep alive the kind of law we saw at work in the early chapters?*

I mean chapters one to four to be a partial response. In them I am trying to think and write in a responsible way as a person of the law. Of course you may spot defects or have larger difficulties with what I do. As I said above, that is all to the good, so long as our argument with each other takes a thoughtful, open-minded, and good faith form, of the kind we can see in law at its best.

I should add that there is nothing magic about the examples developed in those chapters: I could have used any of thousands of statutes or opinions or legal briefs or memoranda, all to much the same effect, that is, to define the life of the law as it has come to exist in our country, and is now subject to systemic threat. The sense of law I am trying to define is likewise not at all unique to me; I think many people trained as lawyers in the last seventy

1. For a sobering read, see Stephen Greenblatt, *Tyrant: Shakespeare on Politics* (2018), in which he explicates the various ways in which Shakespeare in his plays has defined tyranny. The parallels with our situation are telling.

years or so would find it familiar and maybe congenial. Legal education in this country has been a powerful unifying force for the profession.

One way to respond to the deterioration of law and what it means is for us each to try to practice and teach and criticize law in the ways established by our tradition, and to do so as lawyers, as teachers, as judges, or as ordinary citizens. Every effort of that kind is of value. To try to do law in the way in which I have been trying to define it is one response to our situation, and a good one. As long as we can make this effort, we should do so.

But it is possible that we may find ourselves unable to maintain law in that way. Both law and democracy are parts of a larger culture upon which they depend for their intelligibility, their authority, and their efficacy. If that culture changes enough, law and democracy as we have known it may simply become impossible. What are we to do then?

Of course we cannot predict what will happen—maybe in five years law and democracy will be secured in a new and stronger way than ever. I hope so. But it is also possible that they will become less and possible even to imagine, let alone practice. In this last chapter I want to change direction and think a little about what we might try to do and become if that happens, or as it happens. For what is called for in our present situation is not just learning how to do law and democracy in our traditional ways—for that may become impossible—but an effort that is in a sense even more fundamental than that.

One way to put it is to say that in order to live with the dissolution of the law and democracy we have always known and depended upon we need a new and deeper kind of education.

What kind of education? What possibilities should we be trying to realize in ourselves, and how?

To help us think about this question, in this chapter I first look back to a person who lived in a world that was much worse than ours, a world simply without democracy or law or justice as we know these things. I have in mind Augustine of Hippo, who in his own experience of a collapsing world goes through a process of education and change that might help us see possibilities for ourselves that would otherwise be hidden. The heart of his achievement is to recognize deep difficulties that generate new responsibilities.

Augustine was trained not in law but something close to it, namely, rhetoric, an art and profession which he practiced and taught with great success. Gradually he came to see the limits of this life, and his book, the Confessions, *explains where that insight took him. I think he can serve as something of a model for us — not to be slavishly imitated of course, but as a possibility with which to compare who we are becoming as we live the life we have been given.*

In doing this I am moving far from the life of the modern lawyer and citizen. But, as I say, I think Augustine has a lot to teach us about how to live in a deeply unjust world.

After all, he lived under the Roman Empire, which had no democratic justification and no republican structure. He lived through the first sacking of Rome in hundreds of years, which was a frightening demonstration of the fragility of their whole civilization. His own world in Africa was repeatedly marred by intense violence between competing Christian groups.[2] *When he died in 430 C.E., Hippo itself was under siege by the Vandals.*

How does a person of intelligence and decency and moral depth live in such a world? That is the question we will bring to his life and work.

I think that his work in itself offers us an education of a kind that would be most valuable for today's lawyer or citizen. He can help us see what law ought to be, by helping us see what we ought to be, particularly as people who are alive to our own experience of meaning and its limits. I think we might take him, and what he did, as an example for ourselves.

"But he is a religious person, and I am not," someone might say. I think we should be able to learn from him, and take him as a model, whether or not we share his religious commitments. A friend, who is also a distinguished professor of religious studies, once said to me, in response to a question, "I definitely think that religious writers can be read without either dismissing their faith or embracing it;" to which I would like to add, "and I hope without feeling the necessity either to resist it or to yield to it." As you read this part of the chapter ask yourself whether this is true for you.

In the second part of this chapter I discuss a recent play, by François Ost, set in francophone Europe but telling anew the ancient story of Antigone. I think this play presents its readers with kinds of difficulty and responsibility somewhat similar to those Augustine learned to face, and that it can help us see something of the difficulties and responsibilities we ourselves confront. Like the Confessions *it offers us experiences, a set of perceptions and attitudes, that might help us learn how to keep law alive in a new way, even in new and troubling circumstances.*

2. See Brent Shaw, *Sacred Violence: African Christians and Sectarian Hatred in the Age of Augustine* (2011).

I mean this chapter to suggest a way of perceiving and living with and resisting the forces described in chapter five that threaten the integrity and value of law and democracy as we have known them.

LET ME BEGIN BY EXPLAINING how it was that I became engaged with the *Confessions* in the first place. It is a simple story.

Reading Augustine's *Confessions*

In the course of my life I had heard over and over again that the *Confessions* was one of the most important and valuable books in the Western tradition: the first full expression of human inwardness, the deepest actualization of the human self as we have come to know it since, full of depth and mystery. It was said to be fascinating, enlightening, and a true shaper of our culture.

Translations

I started to read the *Confessions,* many times, in many translations, but I found it impossible. I felt I was drowning in an ill-shapen mass of pious platitudes taken from nineteenth-century theologians, who seemed to speak as if their language were not problematic in any way, but simply said what needed to be said, clearly and with the authority of the ages. I could not confidently grasp either the outline or the details of the story.[3]

In these English versions, Augustine seemed to use theological terms in what we lawyers call a "conclusory" way, that is, as though they did not need further elaboration or definition. His psychology likewise seemed elementary and unsophisticated, again as though the subject were one on which his words explained themselves. As for the narrative, that seemed pointlessly complex and substantively trivial. What, for example, is the big deal about stealing pears? It was an adolescent prank, not a serious sin. And so on. Maybe you have had such a response yourself.

None of this helped me discover what his theological language might have meant to him or to see what connections this language might have

3. For an antidote, see Henry Chadwick, *Saint Augustine: Confessions* (1991). For help in reading the *Confessions*, see *A Reader's Companion to Augustine's Confessions* (Paffenroth and Kennedy, eds., 2003). The standard biography is Peter Brown, *Augustine of Hippo* (1967).

with the events of ordinary life, in his era or our own. The whole experience was deeply unsatisfactory. I know other people have had very different responses to the translated Augustine, but this was mine and I saw no way to change it.

Then, about twenty years ago, I revived enough of my high-school Latin to read the first page, and I was, in the modern idiom, blown away.[4] All the impressions I had had of this text were exploded. It was now full of life and immediacy and urgency. Augustine used his terms of theology and psychology, indeed all of his languages, with a constant sense of what they could and could not do, of what they left out or distorted, all in order to say something new and vital. His religious sense was not reducible to theological cliché but was deep, vital, and original.

In recent years I have been able to read the whole thing through, with the help of a Latin teacher, and for me it has become one of the most important books.

The Narrative

The story is that of a very bright provincial boy making his way upward in the world through the power of his mind and tongue, a familiar story to many lawyers today. He starts in an obscure town in North Africa, on the edge of the Atlas Mountains. This is where his education begins, but it quickly takes him to Carthage, the second city of the Western empire, where he studies rhetoric, the queen of disciplines at the time, uniting intellectual skill and practical power. Again, a kind of success that has its contemporary analogue.

He is an academic superstar and becomes a teacher of rhetoric, first in

---

4. Why is the text so much clearer and more powerful in the Latin in which it was composed? This is a complex and important problem, deserving a book of its own. But I can say at least this: that if you are interested in connecting to the mind at work in this text, or any text, you will be far closer to the writer if you can read the words he actually wrote, the words that lived in his mind and in which he composed what he wanted to say. For an analogy think of the difference between reading a poem as it was written, and reading a translation of it into prose, even in English. If you try this you will see that the prose version does almost none of the work of the poem and has almost none of its life. Writers like Augustine are not poets but they are artists, and what they achieve is particular to their language. In a sense his language is one of Augustine's subjects, as he uses and transforms it, criticizing and seeking to improve it. One question to ask of any good writer is "What does she do with (and perhaps to) the language she has inherited?" If she is a good writer, she will be able to accomplish things in her language that simply cannot be achieved in any other.

Carthage, then in Rome. In Milan, the seat of the Empire, he becomes a practitioner of the art, on the staff of the Emperor to whom he personally presents a panegyric. He makes it to a position of power and almost certain wealth. The next step seems to be marriage into a wealthy and powerful family, and perhaps the governorship of a province, with all the wealth and power that implies.

But in Milan, just when an appropriate marriage has been arranged, he goes through a complex intellectual and emotional experience, culminating in his conversion to Christianity, the religion of his mother. He decides to resign his position and to withdraw with some friends to lead a life of philosophical and theological reflection, first in a borrowed villa near Milan, then back in North Africa, where they had all originally come from. On their way home Augustine's mother dies, in Ostia.

At this point the narrative portion of the *Confessions* comes to an end. As I tell it, it may sound like the story of a man who "discovers God" and simply turns his back on the world. But hold on.

Transformations

By the time he wrote the *Confessions*, about 397 C.E., roughly ten years after his return to Africa, it was apparent that Augustine's life had not proceeded according to his plan of religious and philosophical retreat. After three years in Thagaste, his home town, he visited Hippo, a city on the coast, where he was physically forced by a congregation to become a priest against his wishes—they simply would not let him leave the building until he agreed. About five years later, he was made a bishop.

From this point on he was to continue in the active role of priest and bishop—running religious services, giving hundreds of sermons, adjudicating disputes among his flock, carrying on theological wars with those he regarded as heretical—and doing so in a context in which religious difference often led to serious violence.[5]

After the fall of Rome in 410 he was to spend many years writing his magnum opus, *The City of God,* which was simultaneously a comprehensive critique of Roman culture and an equally comprehensive defense of Christianity, made in response to the astonishing and frightening

5. See Brent Shaw, *op.cit.* note 1.

destruction of Roman power. When he died in 430, the Vandals were besieging Hippo, the town where he had lived and worked for decades.

When he began to write the *Confessions* he could already see that his was not really a life of philosophic and religious retreat at all, but a deep and active engagement in the world with all its difficulties, disappointments, and dangers—not a thousand miles away from the life of a busy lawyer today. It is true that he was involved in the church, not the state, but his life was deeply of the world and, in its own way, immensely successful.

This life was deeply different in quality from that other life on which he had first embarked, his life as a teacher of rhetoric. What had changed? This is perhaps the true subject of the *Confessions*, written ten years after the end of the story it tells.

Failure and Conversion

In my experience, autobiographies are often stories of success, but the *Confessions* seems to involve failure after failure, collapse after collapse, not only in Augustine's life but in the very structure of the text.

Thus the narrative is in one sense positive, leading to Augustine's conversion, but in another it is a story of loss of confidence and competence, a kind of dismantling of the self. He starts out with immense confidence in his intelligence, in his ability to understand the world and himself, and in his powers of persuasion, but near the end of the work says, in effect, that the only thing he knows in the world is that God exists, and exists within him.[6] The life that brings him to this point, the life of which he has been telling the story, is in a sense now an unreality, without meaning except for the fact that it brought him to a new way of being.

Let me explain. Before he converted to Christianity, Augustine was a rhetorician with the interests and hopes of a philosopher. First, under the influence of Cicero's *Hortensius*, he discovered philosophy. Then he joined the Manichean religious sect, really on philosophic grounds—he thought they succeeded in explaining the presence of evil in the world by positing not one good and omnipotent God, but two opposed forces: one good, one bad, one light, one dark. But what he was assenting to was for him more a theory than a way of life. His next conversion was

6. "*Et ecce intus eras et ego foris, et ibi te quaerabam*" "Behold, you were within and I outside, where I was searching for you." "*Mecum eras, et tecum non eram*" "You were with me but I was not with you." Book X, chap. i.7.

to Neoplatonism, which again he embraced primarily as a philosophic system, not as a life of religious experience and practice.

In Milan, as he tells it, he had experiences of a different kind, experiences deep in his soul that led him to convert to Christianity and in so doing to abandon the whole philosophic way of understanding the world. In his experience the structure of life based on philosophy breaks down.

Theology breaks down too, at least if theology is thought to be a way of "talking about God." In fact, in the *Confessions,* theology never gets going at all, for in it Augustine never talks *about* God; instead, from the first line to the last, he talks *to* God, the audience addressed in every sentence. The *Confessions* is not a work of theology in the usual sense, then, but a sort of invented genre, a book-length prayer or psalm, which undercuts every other form of thought and imagination in which Augustine or his reader is tempted to engage. In the end, for him there is only Augustine, God, the Scriptures, and the reader.

The question this presents for us is what is left when we have lost what are for us the equivalents of Augustine's rhetoric, Manichaeism, Neoplatonic philosophy, and professional success. What do we still have? Who can we be?

After the Narrative

The first nine books of the *Confessions,* briefly summarized above, are offered as the narrative of Augustine's life; the tenth is a reflection on memory, the eleventh a study of time, and the last two are extensive and imaginative readings of the first few verses of Genesis.

Why does Augustine not simply stop at the end of book nine, when the narrative comes to an end? Does the other material have an important function, and if so, what is it?

I think this material is crucial to the book. One way to put it is to say that in books 1–9 Augustine tells the story of his early life; in books 10–13 he shows how life can be lived, now—by him as he now is, and by the reader as he or she now is. He is in fact not only explaining how life can be lived on these terms, he is showing us how this can be done; and he is not only showing us, he is inviting us to participate in that way of living—a way of living that might be compared with the way of living with the law that I have been trying to embody and stimulate in this book.

Memory

I can put it this way. In book ten Augustine focuses on memory, the central human capacity he has himself been exercising in the first nine books. Thus far he has been telling us what he remembers about his life; in book ten he makes memory itself a problem.

As he presents it, we all start out with the inexplicable and incomprehensible gift of life. Thereafter we use memory constantly, not only when we write the story of our lives as he has been doing, but in leading our lives from day to day. Memory is the embedded experience upon which we rely for everything, from the use of language to the formation of desires to the management of social relations. I think that this is as true for us as it was for him.

And, as he makes us see, memory is profoundly unreliable. In a sense this book is the beginning of his real confession: the confession not of bad things he did as a boy, but of what he has come to know that he does *not* know, even about himself.

What we remember, after all, is not sense data but sense data processed by thought and imagination. Memory is a way of locating ourselves in a process of which we know neither the beginning nor the end, a process that is, in its essential nature, interior and, in a deep way, unverifiable. The "narrative" Augustine has just given us is really just the memory of memories, not a story of facts.

As Augustine comes to realize that all he knows of the world depends upon his memory, which is mysterious, misleading, and incomplete, he also comes to see what is for him the ultimate fact about his knowledge: that all he can be certain of is that God exists and is within him. He is a long way from the bright young man proud of what he knows and of what he can do with his knowledge. Everything except this new knowledge—everything from narrative to autobiography to philosophy to theology—is now buried in the mystery of memory.

Time

In book eleven, Augustine continues this line of thought by reflecting on the mystery of time. His main idea is this: all that is past is no longer real, all that is future is not yet real; so all we have is the present, which is itself not stable but a tiny, infinitesimal razor edge of awareness that disappears as fast as it emerges. In fact, by the time we get to the end of a single word, its beginning is in the past.

The razor edge can be extended slightly through memory and imagination, but it is where we live, in a constantly disappearing present. Again, he would say this is true not only for him, but for us as well. In our terms we might say that he has learned, or tried to learn, to live fully in the present.

To the God to whom he is speaking he says in essence: by an act of inexplicable grace you call upon me, in this edge of time in which I live. That is my only true reality: my presence, your presence, my voice, your voice. On these conditions, nothing else can truly be known. This is the position out of which the *Confessions* is written. The question this presents for us is what we know in our own edge of time, and what we are able and called to do and be.

Augustine is here bringing himself to face both the essential mystery of his own existence and the essential quality of that existence, which is that except for the presence of God within him everything passes away. Nothing else can be held on to and apprehended. Thus it is that in these closing books we find Augustine, who once knew so much, saying again and again, I do not know, I cannot know, this is beyond me.

Though of course many of us do not have the kind of religious experience and understanding upon which Augustine relies so heavily, much of what he says can be seen as true for us today. What we thought we knew when we were younger we no longer know, and we must live with that fact of our experience. The difficulties Augustine faces here have analogues in our lives as well, and in both cases they generate responsibilities.

Genesis

The last two chapters offer a deep and highly imaginative reading of the opening of Genesis, which we can take as showing us a way to live with a central and authoritative text—in this respect very much like a legal text. As I describe the way he reads it, think as well about the readings of American law that were the subject of our first three chapters.

Here the world that Augustine has been creating expands. It now includes not only himself and his God, in the razor edge of the present, but also God's scriptures, his holy word, the reading of which is not simply a matter of seeing the obvious, but, like law in our era, requires an art of reading—an art all the more complex when Augustine recognizes what we too have to recognize, that readings other than his own can be equally true, a fact at which he, perhaps surprisingly, says we should rejoice. He formalizes this position by saying that reading should always proceed on the principle of charity, that is, love of God and love of neighbor—including the neighbor who sees things differently from us.

His reading is driven in part by a desire for truth, in part by an ethic of generosity and charity. This in turn means that his world has expanded to include other people, especially his readers. As a result there is here another transformation, for the community of people engaged in this life of the present is for him the church, the presence of the Spirit in the world.

Do we have something that can serve as an analogue to the book of Genesis in Augustine's life? To his work as a reader of that book?

The Modern Lawyer

As one who has been, by profession, a teacher of law, I cannot help thinking here of the bright young lawyer, familiar to us all, perhaps our own earlier self, the one who structures his or her life by certain objects of ambition: high grades, law review, Supreme Court clerkship, job with a famous and rich firm, early partnership, argument before the Supreme Court, and so forth. This is what Augustine was like, fulfilling his, and his mother's, dream of success. But it all collapsed: philosophy, theology, prestige, power, wealth, even his memory, even his capacity to tell a story. This collapse mirrors the kind of collapse that I think we, in our world, are already starting to experience.

But Augustine's sense of loss has a paradoxical effect, namely, that it gives what he says and thinks an extraordinary immediacy and life, an authenticity and truth, both for himself and for us, almost 1,600 years later. He is wholly in the present, in the present created by this text, and we are too.

Augustine's story is one of benign humiliation, the destruction of his own pretenses and claims, often against his will and without his knowledge, until he is at the end stripped naked and vulnerable and ignorant; but in that condition, he is able to live—and think, and write—in a new and deeper way.

Such are the conditions of life, for him then and for us now. The moment passes: Are we alive in it, to it? Can we speak out of the center of ourselves, aware of what we do not know, what we cannot be? Can our humiliations also be benign? *The Confessions* is written to bring us to the point where such questions are real.

For me the crucial fact of legal practice, as I said in chapter four, is that in this life the language of the law is brought to bear on a series of immediate, unique, and incompletely comprehensible problems in the lives of other people, to which it is the task of the lawyer to do justice—with all the difficulties that term suggests. The lawyer's life is a place where language meets the world. This means that all of his or her learning is suddenly provisional; it is not the source of answers so much as of questions, which have to be newly articulated in the new context that is suddenly at hand. In using the language of the law the lawyer must constantly reformulate it, make it new. The responsibility that such a moment defines is a challenge to mind, character, and imagination. The question is: How are we to meet that challenge in making the meanings we claim for experience—while working, as we do, in a larger community of diverse views? This question is real for us as lawyers today. Can we keep it alive in the future that is to come?

Augustine found a way to work out of his awareness that all learning, all expectations, were provisional only. He not only worked, but worked brilliantly, far better than he would have done had he remained the expert rhetorician he started out to be. The very ephemeral quality of things made it possible for him to be present as mind and imagination in a new and much more complete way to what he was doing. The freshness and newness of life that this transformation entailed gave him immense power, in part because it seems to have erased his earlier susceptibility to embarrassment and his need to impress others.

There is in Augustine a remarkable quality of integrity, which becomes more and more apparent as the external things upon which he at first relied fade away—Cicero's *Hortensius*, Manichaeism, rhetoric, Neoplatonism, and his own confidence in the rightnesss of his views. His openness to the value of readings of Genesis that contradict his own is remarkable in the extreme and rests upon a fundamental humility. If the other person approaches the text with the right spirit, and seeks to learn what can be learned about it, and maintains his own integrity in the process, his words are worthy of respect.

The modern lawyer who tried to learn from Augustine how to become capable of whole-minded thought would find himself or herself trying to create coherence, a project that would never fully succeed; insisting that justice, indefinable as it is, is the ultimate goal of his or her work, and rejecting utterly ways of doing law that reduce it to policy or interest-balancing or some other formulaic mode of thought; living with uncertainty and incoherence of a kind that he or she at one time could not bear; recognizing the value of what those say or do who are also seeking the integrity both of their own minds and of the law, those who are capable of thinking and speaking and writing from the center—the place created as it were by all the other qualities of the existence I describe.

A question for many of us will be how far we can use Augustine as an example, when we do not share his religious commitments and experience.

Of course each of us has to address this question for himself or herself, but my own view is that it is possible to hope to have, as a lawyer, an educative transformation of another sort, without any theological dimension, leading to something like what Augustine comes to attain for himself: that is, an awareness of the evanescence of all things; of the unreliability of memory and intellect; of the essential emptiness of most goals of ambition or competition; of the springs of life and strength within oneself, upon which one may rely; of the hope of speaking always to another as that person is, in that situation at that moment, out of the center of oneself and of one's mind; of the openness of our texts and practices of authority to multiple readings and uses; and ultimately of the power each of us might hope to have of speaking in ways that are true and alive—for only through such speech is justice possible.

Antigone Voilée

I want to close with a brief account of another work, both literary and legal, that is I think of extraordinary interest and importance. I have in mind the version of Sophocles' *Antigone* recently composed by François Ost, professor of law at the University of St. Louis in Brussels.[7]

Entitled *Antigone Voilée* (in English, *Antigone Veiled*), Professor Ost's play locates the Antigone story in a modern European francophone country with a substantial Muslim population—perhaps France, or Belgium. The setting of the events is a highly selective public secondary

7. François Ost, *Antigone Voilée* (2004). The translations are my own. For a fine account of the way Sophocles' play teaches its audience how to engage in the kind of judgment courts have to make when irreconcilable values are in opposition, see Julen Etxabe, *The Experience of Tragic Judgment* (2013).

school, in which Ayisha, the Antigone-figure, and both of her brothers, Nordin and Hassan, and her sister, Yasmina, are students. The two brothers are killed by an explosion of an object apparently in their possession, Nordin immediately, Hassan after a period in the hospital. As the Director of the School sees the facts, this is the fault of Nordin, in his mind a terrorist, who must have been carrying a bomb; Hassan, the good citizen, must have been struggling with him to prevent the use of the bomb when it went off.

The brothers are of course direct parallels to the two brothers of Sophocles' Antigone, who die in battle for the control of Thebes. One of these, Eteocles, is thought by Creon, their uncle (and after the death of Oedipus the ruler of Thebes) to be the good one, dying for the city; the other, Polyneices, is in his view the bad one, attacking the city and seeking to overthrow the government. Eteocles, Creon declares, is to be honored with a public burial; the body of Polyneices is to be thrown out of the city, to be devoured by dogs and birds. Creon announces that it will be a crime punishable by death to provide his body with the protection of religious "burial," which can be achieved simply by sprinkling dust on the body. This is the decree that Antigone disobeys, an act that leads ultimately to her death.[8]

In *Antigone Voilée,* the parallel to the burial of Polyneices is attendance at funeral services for Nordin, to which the Director prohibits any student from going, including Ayisha, who begins to wear the hijab, or veil, in protest. When she is threatened with punishment, she enters upon a fast, from which she ultimately dies.

Much of this play, as of Sophocles' play as well, is taken up with arguments among the various actors about the rightness of the decree in question and of the refusal to obey it. In Ost's play the characters include members of what we would call the board of trustees, including their chair, teachers, a couple of news reporters, as well as the primary antagonists, Ayisha and the Director.

I will not rehearse the arguments except to say that there is surface plausibility in many of them, on both sides. The idea that the school

---

8. Creon's version of the story in the original *Antigone* omits the fact, deep in the tradition, that Eteocles and Polyneices were supposed to share the rule of Thebes in alternate years, and that in the battle in which they were both killed Polyneices was attacking Eteocles—not the city—because Eteocles refused to yield power when his time was up.

should be free to prevent its students from wearing insignia that would divide them on religious lines has of course power, as does the fear that the funeral may become a kind of political theater, challenging the regime of the school. In fact it could be seen to challenge not only the regime of the school but its central educational function. For the mission of a French school, much more clearly than its American counterpart, is to produce citizens who share the national culture in a deep and vital way.

On the other hand, students are allowed to wear crosses and yarmulkes, and small items that indicate belief in Islam, so why not the veil? And the basic factual assumptions upon which the Director is proceeding, namely that Nordin is a terrorist and Hassan a good citizen, are wholly unproven.

As in the original *Antigone,* and as in a good law case too, the arguments not only answer each other, they open up new lines of thought and action. Ayisha starts off being offended by one thing, the prohibition on attending the funeral of her brother, but becomes much more deeply offended by the gradually emerging structures of thought and feeling that underlie that prohibition. This leads to her own theater, of self-starvation.

One beauty of this play is that it brings the mainstream reader or audience to look at this conflict—of course a widespread one in Europe, and present here as well—from the point of view of the Muslim, who is seen by the official world as a threat, and whose willingness to act on her beliefs, even in purely symbolic ways, is seen by some as an offense and a danger, by others very differently indeed.

One line of questioning to which Ayisha is subjected, and which lives for the play's audience as well, is exactly why it is so important for her to wear the veil. Here we naturally want to think legalistically, in terms of rules and sanctions. Does the Qu'ran require it? Upon the threat of what sanctions for disobedience? Or is this just her "personal" idea of what she should do? Or is it really a "cultural" or "political" rather than a "religious" symbol?

What of the argument that the prohibition of the veil is meant to protect the individual girl or young woman from the dehumanizing control of others, especially men, against her own will or preference? If the school permits her to wear the veil, that is, she may be required to do so against her will by members of her community, sometimes under the threat of rape or other forms of violence if she does not. And in any case will the religious affiliation she is enacting in wearing the veil, even if in some sense voluntary, prevent her from ever achieving the condition of autonomy that will permit her to make the authentic choices upon which our idea of democracy and civilization depend?

All this means that the value of the young woman's autonomy is arguably on both sides of the question, not just one. As these arguments and others too are advanced by the various speakers, we come to see how complex and difficult the issue is, especially when regarded not as a matter of law or theory, but of life and action.

We cannot fully evaluate these arguments for we do not know what we think we know, namely what Islam is, or what different versions of it exist; or what the meaning of the veil is—or rather the range of meanings—to Ayisha, to other Muslims, to the world. In this sense these arguments are a call to us to do the work necessary to reaching a right judgment.

But what is a "right judgment"? Think here of Ayisha's own judgment: it is not simply her insistence on wearing the veil that matters, or the persuasiveness of the arguments she makes on her own behalf; it is how she does these things, and who she is in doing so. Some of the arguments advanced against her by time-servers and bullies and administrative cowards have real force (or would have force if they were advanced by others, in another way). The arguments are cogent in themselves, but in the nature of things inconclusive; in the end it is who the proponents are that matters, how they make the arguments they do, and in these respects many of them are contemptible. One can see parallels between these actors, and the way they are judged, with modern lawyers and judges.

In a way that may in fact remind one of the good lawyers described in this book, the most important questions of human life cannot be reduced to proposition or program or external outcome, but lie in the world of character and meaning. Others could do what Ayisha did and be plainly wrong, and the same is true of our own most significant moral judgments: what determines quality at the deepest level is who one is, the meanings one lives by, the way one acts in the world.

So how does the play end? After Ayisha's death the Director realizes something of what he has done, and is ashamed and guilt-ridden. Yasmina, her sister, speaking with authority here, compares this situation with that of her father—Oedipus—when he confronted the Sphinx. He thought he knew more than the Sphinx, Yasmina says. The Director, somewhat puzzled, says he has never seen the Sphinx.

"She was there however, but you didn't see her," says Yasmina:

> You asked questions and made answers. But you didn't think there really were questions. You saw only the answers. You were encumbered with certainties. Answers are easy. All they take is patience and work. But questions are risky. You walk the tightrope above the void, without a safety net. Every step is a disequilibrium. One must believe in the next step, inventing the path as one goes.

The Director asks her if he should resign. Yasmina goes on:

> You still don't understand. Someone else in your place would not have done better than you. It is not a question of being Director or not. It has solely to do with knowing how to listen, how to hear the questions that are posed.

The Director asks whether Nordin is one of the faces of the Sphinx, and Yasmina says: "Yes, and Hassan also."

"And Ayisha?" he asks. "Not she," she replies. "The veil perhaps. You must understand this veil was not a screen, but an enigma. It was not a rejection, rather an appeal, an open question."

"And you?"

Yasmina says, "I have had enough of the questions of others."

The Director turns at the end to thoughts of his son Eric, fearing that he has done something irreparable to himself. Yasmina says, "Certain people are condemned to live. I know something about that."

"What could I ever say to him?"

"There always comes," says Yasmina, "a moment at which you are asked what has been your question. You will have much time now for thinking about your question."

In this play Professor Ost expresses a vision of law, and life, that will be familiar to readers of this book. It is how one lives with the unknown and unknowable, the decisions one makes and the risks one takes, that matters. Life is a series of questions, including the questions this play puts to us. No easy or familiar answer is possible, in law, theology, or life itself. Each of us is responsible for choosing or creating the questions we use to organize our life, the questions that may have the energy and force to carry us into new and unimagined terrain.

What is crucial is the quality of attention we give to the questions we face: the degree to which we have a humility that will permit us to live, like Augustine, with awareness of what we do not know; a capacity to listen, as Ayisha says, to the questions that emerge; and a willingness to stake our lives on the integrity of our responses.

This is true for Ayisha and Yasmina, and true too for the lawyer who feels and accepts the extraordinary responsibilities of her position and her calling, acknowledging the opacity and difficulty of the questions she faces and the importance of the hope they make real.

I have just suggested that in our effort to keep law alive we need not only to continue to practice and teach it in the traditional way that I have been trying to evoke and demonstrate in this book, but to do something else, something in its origin largely internal, something much harder to describe.

The reason it is necessary is that as the culture in which our law and democracy are embedded undergoes transformation, law and democracy will themselves be threatened with analogous transformations, even dissolutions, which we may find it difficult or impossible to perceive. In fact, as I say in chapter five, I think that process has already begun. The law is interwoven with the world in an inescapable way. If we simply continue to practice and teach as we have been taught we may find ourselves increasingly disconnected from the larger culture, irrelevant to other people, and unable to do the very thing we want to do, to keep law alive.

Another way to put this is to say that to keep law alive, in the sense in which I imagine it in the first five chapters of this book, is something we cannot do alone. We need people, lots of people, who also know how to read law, how to speak it, how to imagine it. As those numbers diminish, something else is called for.

What I hope we can learn from our reading of Augustine, who lived in worse times than our own, is that it might be possible for us to achieve changes of perception and understanding that may enable us to live and work in an increasingly corrupted world—changes that may help us rec-

ognize more fully the difficulties we are confronting and the responsibilities they create, and in so doing help us keep a version of law alive as a way of approaching life itself, even if in its institutional forms it withers away.

In this chapter I speak of Augustine, but one could use other examples: Bishop Tutu, for example, or Martin Luther King, or Simone Weil, or Dante, Rosa Parks, or Dietrich Bonhoefer. All of these had a kind of self-knowledge that became a power, a self-sufficiency which made it hard to threaten them, a capacity of the imagination and the heart which gave them strength in the most inhospitable or hostile contexts. They could all speak from the center of themselves and their experience. They all made new questions for themselves. The changes I am talking about are in one sense internal—this is where they begin to happen—but in another sense are external, publicly available, when they are acted upon and made real.

Afterword

AS I SAID IN THE FOREWORD, and as I tried to show especially in chapter five, I think that we are in the midst of a great cultural and political change, which began some time ago and is gaining force. I cannot predict what the outcome will be, but I fear its consequences for the law, as I have been speaking of it. One part of my fear is that the law will change, that we will change, without our really knowing it. I hope that the first few chapters can help us resist our tendencies to ignorance by capturing something of the world we are in danger of losing.

1

This book was written to help keep law alive: especially law in the sense of the complex set of practices—intellectual, social, political, ethical—that I have been describing and portraying. I have not been arguing for the existence of certain rules of law, or even certain fundamental rights of the citizen, but trying to capture something of how law works as an activity of mind and imagination, an activity with possibilities I greatly admire. It is the life of the law itself that I see threatened and want to define.

One problem is that when culture changes we change too, and change in ways we may not be aware of or able to resist. There is no way to avoid it. The question is, how will we change? What phrases, images, slogans, voices will run through our minds and what will we do with them? What will be the associated patterns of feelings, of hopes, and fears? What will we do with them? What expectations will shape our lives? As Ayisha might ask, what will be our questions?

I hope we may be able, at least to some extent, to resist internalizing the changes that are eroding law and democracy and do so by keeping alive in our minds the materials of the law as we have come to know them, in such things as the Model Penal Code and the opinions of Holmes and the Supreme Court's work on race—including our own responses to these things, whether approving or critical.

I do not talk here about such essential ingredients of the rule of law as the principles that laws must always be published, that law should be administered by an independent judiciary, that police should be subject to law, that legal process should be public, and that all of us should be the beneficiaries of a constitutional bill of rights like our own first ten amendments. Of course these, and other principles like them, are crucial. But, as I said in the Foreword, I think they will not mean much in the long run unless law is kept alive in the complex sense in which I mean that term. If that does not happen, these principles will be reduced to forms that have little force and reality.

I don't want to reduce any of this to a set of lessons. The value of what I have done, if any, does not lie in rules or directions, but in an exposure to minds wrestling in deep and genuine ways with their own versions of the problem that besets us.

2

We are not without resources. The question is how we understand and use them.

In an important sense, our world has always been corrupted: think of the hideous institution of human slavery in our country, our criminal genocide of native peoples, the unjust wars we have inflicted on others and ourselves. What we mean by democracy, and constitutional government and the rule of law has always been under threat. We have found ways to live with that fact. The threat is now presented in an especially stark and complete form, but that does not leave us with nothing to do.

If we are lawyers, we can continue to try to teach and to practice law of the kind that is exemplified by the Model Penal Code and the work of Justice Holmes described in chapters one and two. We can continue to insist that law is not rules, not policy, not theory, but an art of confronting and using certain essential and structural tensions, as described in chapter four. We can see it as a way of respecting the authority of legal institutions, and public and private actors within them — a form of respect that can do much to ensure that we also respect the dignity of those to whom law speaks. We can see it as a mode of collective and individual learning. We can, that is, insist upon doing law in the ways I have tried to define in this book, and in doing so find a way to keep it alive — at least so long as there are others who understand that way of doing things, that way of imagining the world.

Every class, every case, in which we insist upon doing real law can be its own act of resistance to the corruption I have described. No one class or case will reverse the course of institutional decay, but if in what we do we can find a way to insist upon our own integrity and the integrity of law, we shall at the least not be contributing to the destruction I see, and may be contributing to its reversal.

3

I think in fact that there are few things that would be better for the world in its present state than to have lots of law teachers teaching law as the art it is, an art that has justice as its constant topic. What is most valuable about our country is not its gross national product, but its constitutional and legal tradition, based as it is upon the idea, never of course fully achieved, of the fundamental equality of human beings — an equality of which we are now losing even the pretense.

But what are we to do, as law and democracy degenerate? To insist so far as we can on our own psychic integrity — the integrity of our thoughts and feelings and actions, of our questions — has its own significance, as testimony and invitation. As I say in chapter five something of this kind is called for in us, if we can define it. I mean my brief readings of Augustine and Ost to show us the way.

In this context I want to say another word about Holmes. In reading *Schenk* again I was struck powerfully once more by the fact that although Holmes treats this as a criminal law case, in doing so, as I say in chapter two, he begins to find a way, "almost without knowing it," to think about the first amendment. This is a crucial moment in the development of law, as it would be in the making of any composition, collective or individual, from history to philosophy to music or painting: the moment, that is, when a person who is engaged deeply and sincerely, and with an open mind, in a practice of thought and imagination finds unconscious resources within the self that produce a new direction, a change in the way the enterprise is imagined. Holmes does that, not by a kind of leap, but by building on his tradition, which he keeps alive as he remakes it.

I think here of the gamelan, an Indonesian musical combination of instruments and musicians, playing for the most part an array of drums and musically resonating tubes. As one listens, an expert once told me, the music goes on in rhythmic and tonal beauty for some time, and then you begin to hear new notes, notes no one is playing, notes that are produced by the harmony itself. This is an image for me of the kind of confident and creative moment that we experience at the beginning of the birth of the first amendment.

Something like this moment is also at work in Augustine's *Confessions*, especially when he comes to recognize at the end his own ignorance and limits, living in a time that is not a dimension, as we normally think of it, but a razor edge of life. I would add François Ost's *Antigone Voilée* as well. These are people who know how to find what is best within themselves and give it public expression, make it part of the larger world.

By them we are offered moments of whole-minded creativity, which provide a ground upon which the culture can be criticized and transformed. This kind of creativity requires an inner stability and openness and hope, which itself requires support from the outer world. It needs a connection with the culture upon which it builds in making its criticisms. It is this kind of moment, crucial to our collective life, that is threatened by the transformation our own world seems to be undergoing. I hope this book can help keep that hope alive.

4

Here I want to return to the article by Sarah Kendzior quoted in the Foreword:

> Authoritarianism is not merely a matter of state control, it is something that eats away at who you are. It makes you afraid, and fear can make you cruel. It compels you to conform and to comply and accept things that you would never accept, to do things you never thought you would do.

> You do it because everyone else is doing it, because the institutions you trust are doing it and telling you to do it, because you are afraid of what will happen if you do not do it, and because the voice in your head crying out that something is wrong grows fainter and fainter until it dies.
>
> We are heading into dark times, and you need to be your own light. Do not accept brutality and cruelty as normal even if it is sanctioned.
>
> That voice is your conscience, your morals, your individuality. No one can take that from you unless you let them. They can take everything from you in material terms – your house, your job, your ability to speak and move freely. They cannot take away who you truly are. They can never truly know you, and that is your power.
>
> But to protect and wield this power, you need to know yourself—right now, before their methods permeate, before you accept the obscene and unthinkable as normal.[1]

Finally, I want to recall what my friend the rabbi said about knowing Jewish law, when I asked, "Does someone know the law when he can repeat the rules that tell him what to do? Or when he can engage in the activity of reading them, separately or in conjunction with each other, and applying them sensibly to new circumstances? Is even that enough?" As I said earlier, my friend said it was not: he must know who he is in relation to the law, both as an individual and as a member of a people; this means that he must know that this law is part of a covenant with the God of Israel and he must understand the story that connects that God with this people. In particular he or she must recognize that this law was given to the Hebrew people just after their escape from slavery, at the moment when they attained the free and autonomous state that made them capable of receiving the simultaneous gift and restraint of law.

Something like this is what this book has been driving at from the beginning. We must know who we are in relation to the law, both as the makers of it, as lawyers whose task is to keep it alive, and as citizens acting through representative democracy; we must know that our law, and the Constitution that lies behind it, are great events in the history of

1. Sarah Kendzior, "We Are Heading into Dark Times," *De Correspondent*, November 18, 2016.

humanity, a huge experiment, as Lincoln said. But we may also need to find ways to come to terms with its degeneration and loss.

Our law is not only an achievement but a gift, a gift that both assumes and makes possible our freedom. It is a gift made in the hope that as free people we can rise to the challenge of living with the law, which has done so much to make us who we are. Now we face the challenge of living without it.

5

This book is driven by love of something that seems now to be under threat. I do not want to lose it. This is a moment, before it changes or goes entirely, when we can see it, and hear it, and think about it, perhaps more clearly than we could before the threat occurred. I hope I have managed to say something useful about what makes the law so vital, interesting, and important to us all. My aim in this book has to been to give to the law, and to the culture of which it is a part, a voice that might be heard even in a different world.

Works Cited

Note: "n" designates footnote.

Aleinikoff, Alex, "Constitutional Law in the Age of Balancing," 62n

Alvarez, Jose, "Torturing the Law," 123n

Brown, Peter, *Augustine of Hippo*, 138n

Campbell, Michael C., "African Genetic Diversity," 75n

Chadwick, Henry, *St. Augustine: Confessions*, 138n

Chafee, Zechariah, "Freedom of Speech in War Time," 4n, 36n, 37n

Clark, Rodney, "Racism as a Stressor for African Americans," 57n

Cone, James, *The Cross and the Lynching Tree*, 56n

Cooper, Frederick, *Beyond Slavery*, 59n

Cover, Robert M., *Justice Accused*, 63n

Danner, Mark, *Torture and Truth*, 123n

Davis, David Brion, "Looking at Slavery from Broader Perspectives," 53n

Davis, David Brion, "Slavery—White, Black, Christian, Muslim," 53n

Edin, Kathryn and Luke Shaefer, *$2 a Day, Living on Almost Nothing in America*, 110n

Extabe, Julen, *The Experience of Tragic Judgment*, 147n

Foley, Neil, *The White Scourge*, 52n

Frost, Robert, "The Figure a Poem Makes," 102n

Genovese, Eugene, *Roll, Jordan, Roll*, 53n

Gibson, Margaret A., *Minority Status and Schooling*, 57n

Green, Thomas A., *Freedom and Criminal Responsibility in American Legal Thought*, 18n

Greenblatt, Stephen, *Tyrant*, 135n
Heschel, Abraham Joshua, *The Sabbath*, 4n
Holmes, Oliver Wendell, *The Common Law*, 31
Holt, Thomas, *The Problem of Race in the 21st Century*, 52n, 60n, 66n
James, S.A., "John Henryism and the Health of African Americans," 57n
Johnson, Charles S., *Growing Up in the Black Belt*, 59n
Kendzior, Sarah, " We Are Heading into Dark Times," xvii, 159n
Kinder, Donald R., *Divided by Color*, 60n
Kousser, J. Morgan, "The Shaping of Southern Politics," 59n
Larue, L.H., "Stories vs. Theories," 46n
Lempert, Richard, "The Force of Irony," 65n
Luban, David, "Difference Made Legal: The Court and Dr. King," 50n
McPherson, James M., *Battle Cry of Freedom*, 54n
Mendelson, Nina, "A Control-Based Approach to Shareholder Liability," 70n
Model Penal Code, 10–21 *passim*, 29–30
Molnar, Stephan, *Human Variation, Races, Types, and Ethnic Groups*, 74n
Myrdal, Gunnar, *An American Dilemma*, 59n
Nagel, Robert F., *Constitutional Cultures*, 62n
Novick, Sheldon M., *Honorable Justice: The Life of Oliver Wendell Holmes*, 36n
Offer, Avner, *The Challenge of Affluence*, 111n
Ost, François, *Antigone Voilée*, 147–152 *passim*
Paffenroth and Kennedy, eds., *A Reader's Companion to Augustine's Confessions*, 138n
Petuchowski, Jakob, "*Ever Since Sinai*," 4n
Pildes, Richard, "Democracy, Anti-Democracy, and the Canon," 59n, 66n
Polenberg, Richard, *Fighting Faiths*, 28n, 36n
Posner, Richard A., "Pragmatism Versus Purposivism," 119n
Powell, Jefferson and James Boyd White, eds., *Law, Democracy, and the Empire of Force*, 108n
Powell, Jefferson, *Targeting Americans*, 124n
Raban, David, *Free Speech in its Forgotten Years*, 24n

Rodeiger, David, *Towards the Abolition of Whiteness*, 52n
Shaefer, Luke and Kathryn Edin, *$2 a Day, Living on Almost Nothing in America*, 110n
Shakespeare, William, *Troilus and Cressida*, 128n
Shaw, Brent, *Sacred Violence*, 137n, 140n
Sidney, Sir Philip, *The Defense of Poesie*, 101n
Simpson, A.W. Brian, "The Common Law and Legal Theory," 100n
Soper, Philip, *An Ethics of Deference*, 118n
Takaki, Ronald, *Strangers from a Different Shore,* 53n
Third London Airport Commission, "Report," 125n
Thompson, Chalmer E., "Racism, Mental Health, and Mental Health Practice," 57n
Twain, Mark, *Huckleberry Finn*, 46–48, 74
Wechsler, Herbert, "Toward Neutral Principles of Constitutional Law," 61n, 76n
Weil, Simone, "L'Iliade ou la poème de la force," 114n
West, Robin, *Progressive Constitutionalism* 64n, 70n
Wharton, Francis, *A Treatise on Criminal Law*, 30n
White, James Boyd and Jefferson Powell, eds., *Law, Democracy, and the Empire of Force*, 108n
White, James Boyd, *Acts of Hope*, 116n; *From Expectation to Experience*, 111n; *Heracles' Bow,* 8n, 16n, 90n; *Justice as Translation*, 65n, 119n; *Living Speech*, xiv, 116n; *The Edge of Meaning,* 43n, 47n; *The Legal Imagination*, 46n, 53n, 72n, 87n, 97n, 126n, 130n; *When Words Lose Their Meaning*, 90n, 113n, 133n
Woodward, C. Vann, *The Strange Career of Jim Crow*, 59n, 66n

Cases Cited

Note: "n" designates footnote.